"George Whalin's insightful new book, *Retail Success!* makes good on its tall-order promise to help the reader 'increase sales, maximize profits, and wow customers.' He has parlayed a career as a distinguished retail observer and commentator into a must-read book for retailers. Anyone who reads his book will come away excited about improving their business and armed with clearly laid out, practical ways to get it done."

—GARRETT BOONE, Chairman
The Container Store

"A practical road map for current and future retailers who want to offer their customers even more than a worthwhile shopping experience. George Whalin hits the mark with great perspective and inspires us all to make something great even greater."

—KIP TINDELL
CEO and President
The Container Store

"George Whalin possesses a profound understanding of retail business. He is the foremost authority on the competitive environment, the value of brand and product, and the required operational fundamentals necessary to thrive in today's retail world."

—MARK KING, President
Taylor Made/adidas Golf

"Practical advice from one of America's most knowledgeable retail observers."

> —DR. LEONARD L. BERRY
> *Author of* Discovering the
> Soul of Service

"I think that anyone who is serious about retailing or more to the point...being a premier retailer should read this book. We need tools to help us evaluate ourselves, our customers, and our competition, and this is a great one."

> —MARK BURRIS
> *Elliott's Hardware Inc.*

"Attention retailers: Your only guide to the new challenges of the 21st century, *Retail Success!* All the latest issues are covered with great insights that are brilliant!"

> —DAN L. BERNSTEIN, CEO
> *Patti's Hallmark Gold Crown Stores*

"*Retail Success!* is a valuable addition to any retailer's bookshelf, an enlightening compilation of the thoughts and views of one of our industry's best, a treasure of helpful insight, with a peek into the future."

> —DOUGLAS E. RAYMOND
> *President & CEO*
> *Retail Advertising & Marketing*
> *Association*

"George is...no-nonsense...with advice for practical ways to drive retail sales. Our Hallmark Gold Crown retailers have benefitted from his advice."

—*CAROL HALLQUIST*
Vice President, Specialty Retailing
Hallmark Cards

"Your book set off the entrepreneurial bent in me, and I could not put it down...I knew you were renowned for your retail acumen, but the depth and breadth of your research, knowledge, and experience is truly impressive. Any retailer who reads this book in the spirit of learning more about retailing will come away on a new 'high' that can make their business more exciting and profitable."

—*CARL F. PAUL, CEO*
Golfsmith International, L.P.

"*Retail Success!* is a must read for anyone who wants to be successful in retailing, whether it be an owner, manager, or someone just starting out in the retail business. You cover every detail succinctly in an easy to read and understand writing style."

—*FRANK PAUL, President*
Golfsmith International, L.P.

"As I read your new book, *Retail Success!* I was amazed how you covered so many important points of running a retail operation in such a concise, effective way...I have never found such a useful book full of guidelines and ideas that really do work. This book is a must for new as well as experienced managers and owners and also provides a very useful tool for creating effective management and employee motivational and informative meetings."

—*DIANE POWERS*
Owner/Operator
Bazaar Del Mundo

"This book is a must read if you're a store manager or the CEO of a retail operation. This book has tremendous take home value."

—*MITCHELL B. MODELL*
President/CEO
Modell's Sporting Goods

"George is the eyes and ears of my customers. He has a way of drawing you into the retail confessional and making you examine how you're conducting your business. *Retail Success!* is packed with common sense and extraordinary ideas. I'll keep it handy as a reference on my desk."

—*NICK MOKELKE*
General Manager
Cog Hill Golf and Country Club

"*Retail Success!* offers insight, wisdom, and fresh and actionable ideas that make me determined to be better at my craft."

—WYNN FERREL, Owner
Ferrel's Hallmark Shops

"A book that every retailer should read, as well as his or her sales staff. It not only gives the basics to good retailing but also gives new ideas and direction for you to strive for greater success. It is easy reading. This book can shake up your thinking about what retailing will become in the next few years."

—DON PFAU
Chairman of the Board
Sports Inc.

"We believe every retailer could improve their business by reading and adopting some of your retail ideas."

—EDWIN and RONNIE WATTS, Owners
Edwin Watts Golf

"This book delivers as promised. George Whalin is an astute observer and chronicler of cutting edge developments and best practices in retailing. He goes beyond survival and demonstrates how to thrive at retail with enthusiasm!"

—D. CHRISTOPHER DAVIS
Chief Executive Officer
World Floor Covering Association

"The challenge for today's retailer is to find the balance between seeing the 'big picture' and the truism that 'retail is detail.' [*Retail Success!*] should help every retailer find this balance. From Chapter 2 on distinguishability (the big picture) to Chapter 19 on advertising (detail), George Whalin gives concrete examples to help retailers find success."

—*H. JAMES BAUM, Owner*
Baum's Inc

"George always boils it down to the basics. He always brings you back to the reality that doing what's best for the customer is the secret to success."

—*RICK LILLIE, Vice President*
PGA Tour Shops

"Truly the framework for any successful retailer. Very factual 'block and tackling' while prodding the imaginary creative thinker to operate outside the box. Excellent reading with sparkles of enthusiasm!"

—*DAVID L. KRIEGEL, President*
Drug Emporium

"Our company uses the 15-minute daily meeting. *Retail Success!* will be my new handbook. I think readers will be anxious to digest each chapter."

—*MARION HALFACRE*
Traditional Jewelers

"... a concise, easy-to-read, wonderfully arranged narrative from which every retailer can benefit! I couldn't put it down, and I wholeheartedly recommend it. Congratulations on another great service to this industry."

—*MICKEY MOORE, President*
Texas Retailers Association

"George Whalin captures the essence of what it takes to grow and survive in today's fragmented and competitive retail environment."

—*LAURIE HUDSON, President*
Platinum Guild International
USA Jewelry Inc.

"*Retail Success!* is a fascinating collection of practical, hands-on ideas and solutions that challenge retailers. In today's highly competitive retail environment, a retailer must develop and execute a total strategy for success."

—*PATRICK K. HICKS, President*
Kentucky Grocers Association, Inc.

"Your book has so many great ideas that as I read it, it truly has helped me realize that we have many things to work on to achieve our everyday goals to be 'the best of the best.'"

—*CARL E. ROSE*
Carl's Golfland

"*Retail Success!* is a practical and useful quick read for time-pressured retailers who seek guidance to help solve everyday business challenges. It is a must for every retailer's bookshelf."

—JAMES L. FALTINEK
President & CEO
National Sporting Goods Association

"I have been a big fan of George Whalin's teachings for many, many years. He is the all-time master of what it takes to be successful in retailing. After reading his new book, I became very excited about applying the principles of *Retail Success!* I can't wait to get the book into the hands of all our store owners and their managers."

—MERLIN HAYES
Chairman of the Board
HobbyTown USA

"George's new book is filled with his 'take' and advice on many topics that are more timely than ever for retailers. [He] has some great observations and valuable insights into some of today's key business topics."

—BURT SQUIRES
Corporate V.P. Stores
Dillards

"In *Retail Success!* author and consultant George Whalin chronicles the retail industry's evolution from the perspective of a customer, giving even the most polished retailers an alarming account of why shoppers return to their stores or abandon. Bravo!"

—LORRIE GRANT
Retail Reporter
USA Today

"This is a great book and written so it can be read, digested, and acted on quickly."

—BILL BOETTGE, President
National Shoe Retailers Association

"Certainly one of the most comprehensive studies of retail today—easy to find topics, easy to read, and easy to pack in a briefcase!"

—BILL HAYMOND
Vice President, National Accounts Sales
Pioneer Electronics

"Any company that can Wow its customers is bound to succeed. Your book is a terrific how-to guide for all of us aspiring to get to Wow."

—MICHAEL OWEN, President
Barr Display

RETAIL SUCCESS!

RETAIL SUCCESS!

*Increase Sales, Maximize Profits, and
Wow Your Customers in the Most
Competitive Marketplace in History!*

GEORGE WHALIN

WILLOUGHBY
PRESS

This publication is designed to provide accurate and authoritative information in regard to the subject matter covered. It is sold with the understanding that the publisher is not engaged in rendering legal, accounting, or other professional services. If legal advice or other expert assistance is required, the services of a competent professional should be sought.

Permission to reproduce or transmit any portion of this book in any form or by any means, electronic or mechanical, including photocopying and recording, or by an information storage and retrieval system, must be obtained by writing to the publisher at the address below.

Willoughby Press
1635 S. Rancho Santa Fe Road, Suite 206
San Marcos, California 92069

First Edition. Published 2001
Printed in the United States of America
5 4 3 2

Library of Congress Card Number 00-1111034

ISBN 0-9706435-0-0

In loving memory of

Gina Whalin
A Nordstrom All-Star

CONTENTS

◆

AVOIDING TRIAL AND TERROR

I f you look at the graduates of the five leading business schools in the US over the past fifty years and look at the first job graduates took with their new MBA in hand, only a tiny percentage went to retail companies.

Retail for the last millennia has been something people discovered they had in their blood. Whether brilliant merchant or plodding vendor, retail demanded a special commitment. At any level the only thing guaranteed was hard work.

◆

The point of entry, if it wasn't through family, was often by accident. A part-time job that turned full-time. Discovering a flair or talent for something that precipitated the need to trade. For many senior executives the retail job offer came as a sideways career move. For many small merchants the step into the retail abyss came from the desire to work for themselves. However, running a store or a chain of stores is harder than it looks from the outside. Giving good store means understanding layout and merchandising. It means being able to lead and inspire employees. It means delivering on your promise to the customer consistently day after day.

Being a good merchant has never been easy. The great merchants of the twentieth century learned the details of their craft the hard way—by doing it. They succeed by guts, instinct, and ability to stay focused. If they were lucky, they had a mentor. Someone who brought insight out of chaos. Someone who was willing to teach and help revisit the fundamentals. Someone who could look and listen. For every merchant or aspiring merchant who has missed having that personal mentor, there is George Whalin.

Unlike Columbia Business School professors, George never uses a twenty-five cent word when a nickel word would do just fine. There are no flow charts or fancy three-dimensional diagrams. George dispenses plain and straightforward good advice. From small comic book store owners to the CEO of giant retail chains, George has been a mentor, coach, and cheerleader. In person, George inspires calm and confidence. He's old enough and gray enough to inspire trust and yet he has an easy laugh and melodious voice that is a pleasure to listen to. In this new book, that sonorous and easy tone comes right through the printed words on the page.

If you are in retail, time never comes to you in big chunks. You get breaks, some when you are bone weary, others when you just need to hide for a few minutes. Believe me, George understands. To be honest, you don't have to read this book cover to cover. You don't have to start at the beginning. You can flip and surf, dip and sip. But if you have anything to do with retail, I do recommend that you get to know George and this book is a great place to start.

—*PACO UNDERHILL*
Author of Why We Buy

ACKNOWLEDGEMENTS

◆

This book is the result of a lifetime devoted to the study of retailing and how to sell to and serve customers. It is also the result of the opportunities I've had during my career to learn from some exceptionally savvy people.

My first mentor was Maury Silverman. Maury had spent more than 40 years as a retailer by the time I worked for him. He built a substantial business during a time when there were no computers and very few books or college classes to help guide or influence a retailer's thinking. In those days, even one small mistake could put you out of business. Maury taught me the most important fundamentals of retailing—how to keep the store looking neat and orderly, how to make every customer feel welcome, and how to pay absolute attention to the details.

◆

My second mentor was Andy Zerbo, an automobile salesman who accidentally found himself in the retail business. Andy taught me how to think like a merchant and sell as though my life depended on it. He also taught me the importance of treating every single customer as if they were my only customer.

Both these men were extraordinary and had a great passion for retailing. They also had the patience necessary to teach and guide a young man through his early career in retailing. I am forever grateful for their efforts.

By 1987, when I started Retail Management Consultants, I had spent 25 years of my life in retail. I falsely believed I had amassed a significant amount of expertise and insight into this business. Little did I know that from that day forward I would learn a thousand times more than I had during the previous twenty-five years.

And I have learned every bit as much from my clients and audiences as they, hopefully, have learned from me. I want to thank all the retail executives and owners who invited me into their stores, shared their successes and failures, and helped me learn about this industry.

This book would not exist if it were not for the efforts of my amazing wife and business partner, Terri Pilot. Business books are nearly always a collaborative effort and *Retail Success!* is no exception. Terri not only was a valuable collaborator for the book you hold in your hands, but also the editor and graphic designer. During its writing, she challenged my assumptions and helped bring the words to life.

She took my thoughts and made sense out of what I wanted to say. I could not have done it without her.

Special thanks go to Greg Wiezorek, who also helped with the editing process. He smoothed over the bumps and added clarity to my sometimes clumsy and always conversational writing style.

Thanks also go to one of retailing's most insightful experts—Paco Underhill—for writing the foreword to this book. I am grateful for the opportunities I've had to learn from him.

I hope you find *Retail Success!* as enjoyable and insightful to read as it was for me to write.

—*GEORGE WHALIN*

CHAPTER
1

REVOLUTIONARY RETAILING

Since the mid-1980s when I started my consulting business, I've visited thousands of stores. In my continuing effort to learn what makes great retail businesses great, I have had the chance to analyze hundreds of retail companies. I've seen some truly revolutionary retail businesses that have chosen paths to success using an entirely different approach from everyone else.

Retail companies such as Home Depot, Bed Bath &

Beyond, and The Container Store have built their businesses by offering massive selections in equally massive super-stores. The Body Shop, Disney, Hard Rock Cafe, and Harley Davidson stores have built their businesses around their own unique branded merchandise.

A number of revolutionary retail organizations have become successful under the guiding hand of charismatic and visionary leaders. This certainly is true of Gallery Furniture based in Houston, Texas. This high-volume single store reflects the clear vision, powerful leadership, and charisma of Jim "Mattress Mac" McIngvale. And, of course, much of the success Starbucks has enjoyed is a direct result of the vision of leader Howard Schultz.

Conventional retailers build their businesses around tried-and-true concepts. Revolutionary retailers go in a completely different direction. Anita Roddick, founder of The Body Shop chain, was once quoted as saying, "I watch where the cosmetics industry is going and then walk in the opposite direction." This kind of thinking is common to those who create revolutionary retail companies.

IT ISN'T JUST ABOUT CREATING A NEW FORMAT!

Over the last few years there have been a small number of retailers who actually defined their businesses around a revolutionary approach to selling merchandise. For example, Sol Price created the first of an entirely new retail concept when he opened the original Price Club in San Diego. And Sam Walton literally wrote the book on general merchandise discount store retailing.

Creating a new retail format in today's marketplace, however, is a rare occurrence. Most revolutionary retailers build their businesses around unique merchandise, unusual locations, entertainment- or theme-oriented shopping environments, or pressing customer needs.

IT'S NOT EASY!

A revolutionary concept by itself is not always enough. During the counter-culture days of the late 1960s and early 1970s, *Whole Earth Catalog* began in Berkeley, California, by offering merchandise that fit the needs of those consumers who lived what was then called an alternative lifestyle. The great success of the *Whole Earth Catalog* spawned a small chain of Whole Earth Access stores around the San Francisco Bay Area.

For many years the company flourished, and the original Berkeley store became one of the area's best-known retail destinations, attracting visitors from all over the world. However, in 1996, the last of the Whole Earth Access stores closed. The customers had changed, the marketplace had changed, and the company failed to adapt to the changes. But the major problem plaguing Whole Earth in later years was poor management. Without sound business practices and a customer base to support the concept, Whole Earth Access failed.

TOWER RECORDS

In 1960, Russ Solomon, another revolutionary retailer, opened the first Tower Records store in Sacramento, California, and a few years later he opened his first music superstore on Columbus Street in San Francisco. Today, the company operates stores all across the United States, in Japan, and in Europe. Tower's eCommerce site is one of the most shopped music and video sites on the Web. This revolutionary company is not owned by some giant conglomerate, and as of this writing, the company's shares are not publicly traded. Tower is still owned and managed by Russ Solomon. What makes Tower Records revolutionary today is the same thing that made it revolutionary when I was buying records as a teenager in northern California. Tower Records offers a great selection of music in every single category at a fair price.

A REVOLUTIONARY T-SHIRT RETAILER!

Another revolutionary retail company that grew from the apparel habits of young people in the 1960s is Crazy Shirt based in Honolulu, Hawaii. When Rick Ralston opened his first Crazy Shirt store in the International Marketplace in Waikiki, he was selling hand-painted and airbrushed T-shirts. At the time, this newly exposed apparel item was still considered underwear. Ralston's Crazy Shirt stores led the way for thousands of other imprinted T-shirt stores around the world. But instead of becoming just like everyone else, the Crazy Shirt stores, usually located in tourist areas, still feature high-quality merchandise, their own innovative designs, and great customer service.

A REVOLUTIONARY INDEPENDENT!

Another approach to revolutionary retailing is being executed by a two-store supermarket operation in Dayton, Ohio. While there certainly are other revolutionary food stores around the country including Stew Leonard's stores in Connecticut and New York, and Trader Joe's based in Pasadena, California, there aren't any quite like Dorothy Lane Market. Owner Norman Mayne overwhelms customers with reasons to shop in his stores.

They have cooking classes, monthly wine lovers and seafood lovers newsletters, a sushi bar, a frequent-buyer program called The Club DLM. They have a new Spa Store that features vitamins, herbs, and body-care products as well as a whole range of great products from the store's own bakery including Killer Brownies® and an incredible wine and cheese department.

Taking advantage of technology, customers can take a look at the sushi bar menu, read the latest issue of the wine newsletter, search the store's recipe archives, and even order some world-famous Killer Brownies® on the company's Web site. All this might not seem quite so revolutionary if Dorothy Lane Market was a large national chain, but this is a family-owned business with two stores in Dayton, Ohio.

REVOLUTIONARY CONCEPTS!

For some, it started with a revolutionary concept that over the years was leveraged to build a successful business. In the case of Golfsmith International, based in Austin, Texas, the concept was to supply do-it-yourselfers with the equipment, tools, components, and instructions needed to make golf clubs. In addition to being the leading company in the component business, Golfsmith operates an extremely successful catalog and a fast-growing chain of golf specialty stores.

Superstores are now commonplace even in the smallest towns, but before anyone had ever heard of a superstore, Nebraska Furniture grew to become one of the nation's best-known stores of any kind by offering a massive selection of moderately priced furniture. Nebraska Furniture Mart, now owned by billionaire investor Warren Buffet, is still a revolutionary retail business. Its 75-acre campus includes the more than 200,000-sq.-ft. furniture showroom along with a 102,000-sq.-ft. Mega Mart that features massive selections of appliances, consumer electronics, and entertainment products. The complex also includes Mrs. B's Clearance & Factory Outlet (named after the company's well-known founder and legendary furniture retailer Rose Blumkin.)

SO WHAT DO THEY HAVE IN COMMON?

Revolutionary retailers have some very important characteristics in common:

- They don't fit into anyone's mold.

- They're different from all their competitors.

- They revel in going the opposite direction from other retailers, particularly those in their same merchandise specialty.

Revolutionary retailers are the ones who make retailing such a dynamic and interesting business.

DISTINGUISHABILITY: KEEPS CUSTOMERS COMING BACK

N ot far from my office is a 1.2-sq.-mile shopping area that includes a major regional mall along with nine strip centers of varying sizes. Shoppers can choose from eight major department and discount stores including two Macy's, a Wal-Mart, Target, Sears, Robinson's-May, JCPenney, and scores of specialty stores—396 in all!

How can any one store stand out in such an overcrowded

marketplace? Retailers everywhere are concerned about the over-storing of America, but the competitive environment in local towns and communities is most overwhelming because of this kind of staggering concentration of stores all vying for the same consumers. How can an apparel store capture the attention of prospective customers when 50 others are within walking distance? What can a shoe store do to bring customers in when there are 31 others trying to do the same thing? The answer? Distinguishability!

CREATING DISTINGUISHABLE STORES

One strategy some retailers have embraced to distinguish their stores from the competition is to create visually dynamic environments. The growing number of entertainment and theme-oriented retailers like Warner Bros. Studio Stores and NikeTown has changed what customers expect from their shopping experiences. Consumers have seen it all—from spectacular graphics and video walls to basketball courts, animated cartoon characters, and in-store DJs.

Among my favorite knock-your-socks-off stores are the Seattle, Washington; Bloomington, Minnesota; and Denver, Colorado, REI stores. They are designed to grab the customers' attention before they even get into the store. Stark, modern, and eye-catching on the outside, they are warm, comfortable, and inviting on the inside. Whether a customer is interested in backpacking, climbing, hiking, bicycling, or mountaineering, REI provides the opportunity to try both hardware and apparel in the store before buying, all adding to the experience. They are in the business of selling experience-related merchandise, so it's only natural they would offer their customers an experience-related shopping environment.

Another of my favorite experience-oriented retailers is FAO Schwartz—specifically the Las Vegas, Nevada, and Orlando, Florida, stores. Before you get through the doors of the Las Vegas store, you are faced with a huge, two-story Trojan horse. In Orlando, there's a giant Raggedy Ann doll in the front. These stores are fun, exciting, stimulating, and, most important of all, memorable.

Toys and sporting goods aren't the only merchandise categories that can be sold in dramatic environments. The spectacular Crate & Barrel store on Chicago's Michigan Avenue is visually dynamic both inside and out. And the newest Jordan's Furniture stores in Massachusetts are without a doubt among the most dramatic and memorable furniture stores anywhere in the world.

One of the challenges of today's massive superstore formats is to create a space that's big enough to show lots of merchandise and, at the same time, provide a comfortable, even intimate, shopping environment. No easy task. With massive stores of more than 100,000 square feet, Barry and Elliot Tatleman, owners of Jordan's Furniture, have done exactly that.

A CONSTANTLY CHANGING MIX OF UNIQUE AND INTERESTING MERCHANDISE!

Another way to create distinguishable stores is by offering a constantly changing mix of unique and interesting merchandise. California-based Restoration Hardware, with stores in regional malls around the country, does this about as well as any retail chain anywhere. What you see upon entering is much more than a hardware store. It's a furniture store, gardening store, home decorating store, cooking store, gift store, and bookstore. The company does sell some decorative hardware items, such as drawer pulls and cupboard handles, but hardware represents only a small percentage of the merchandise selection. Add terrific presentation and friendly people and the result is incredible customer loyalty and tremendous growth in just a few short years.

DESTINATION STORES

But it's not just fast-growing, publicly held retail chains that are able to offer customers a constantly changing mix of unique and interesting merchandise. In the small Midwest town of Atchison, Kansas, Mary Carol Garrity operates Nell Hill's, an extraordinary home furnishings store. If you were to ask a real estate expert to pick the ideal location for a home furnishings store that offers merchandise to discerning, upscale consumers, Atchison, Kansas, would not be the place! And unless you are one of the 11,000 or so residents who live in Atchison or one of the small rural towns nearby, you'll have to drive at least an hour just to get to the store. Since most of the merchandise (95 percent) goes to homes 50-plus miles away in the Kansas City area, Nell Hill's certainly fits the description of a destination store.

With an exceptional mix of furniture and home decorating accessories rivaling that of any store anywhere, Mary Carol Garrity proves every day that customers will drive miles and miles to buy unique and interesting merchandise. A visit to Nell Hill's is a great adventure. You'll see merchandise that just isn't available in most malls, chain stores, or catalogs. To keep customers coming back, Mary Carol and her staff completely overhaul the store—bringing in new merchandise, creating new displays, and reorienting the store—about every eight weeks.

ABC Carpet & Home, located in a city with such great stores as Zabar's, Berghdorf Goodman, and the Macy's and Bloomingdale's flagship stores, has become one of New York City's best-known shopping destinations. The 100-year-old carpet and home furnishings retailer does business in two buildings located in the city's Flatiron District. In 350,000 square feet of selling space, ABC Carpet & Home offers furniture, antiques, rugs, carpeting, home textiles, and accessories. Paulette and Evan Cole and their 500-plus capable associates serve the needs of over a million very picky customers each year in one of the most competitive marketplaces anywhere in the world. What makes ABC

Carpet & Home distinguishable is their massive selection of high quality, constantly changing, unique, and interesting merchandise.

DISTINGUISHING THE STORE WITH KNOWLEDGEABLE, FRIENDLY ASSOCIATES!

Distinguishable retail businesses also place a high priority on staffing their stores with friendly, knowledgeable associates who genuinely care about serving customers. Over the last several years, a great deal has been written about the importance of great customer service (see Chapter 8). Fortunately or unfortunately, depending on your perspective, the message has been all but ignored by a good many retailers.

One of those who hasn't ignored the importance of great customer service is Abt Electronics & Appliance, a one-store company located in the Chicago suburb of Morton Grove. The store, owned and managed by Bob Abt, is surrounded by such big chains as Circuit City, Best Buy, and Sears. And while other independent electronics and appliance stores have gone out of business in record numbers, Mr. Abt's one-store operation grew from a 2,000-sq.-ft. store in the 1980s to a 130,000-sq.-ft. superstore with an adjoining 80,000-sq.-ft. warehouse today.

Abt offers a massive selection of top name electronics and appliances in a very well-merchandised environment, but it's the store's sales associates, cashiers, and delivery people who execute Mr. Abt's commitment to outstanding service. In the Chicago area, Abt service is legendary, and because of that, Bob Abt has been able to distinguish his single store from all the rest.

OPPORTUNITIES FOR RETAILERS WHO WANT TO BE DIFFERENT!

Visit stores in any shopping center in the country and you will see far too many that look the same, sell the same merchandise, and treat customers with indifference. What's most exciting about retailing today is the small number of retailers, large and small, who understand the value of being different. They know that to stand out, they must offer unique merchandise, provide their customers with an environment that is interesting and exciting, and always deliver a shopping experience that is pleasant and memorable.

◆

CHAPTER 3

GREAT STORES DON'T HAPPEN BY ACCIDENT

S uccessful retailing has always been about selling lots of merchandise. In order to sell a lot of merchandise, stores must be visually interesting, well-conceived, and easy to shop. They must be merchandised to fit the customer, the category, and the community. And the merchandise must be the star.

Making the merchandise the star requires an almost obsessive approach to creating exactly the right environment so

◆

the merchandise always is well-presented and attractive to customers. I have scrutinized some of the best-conceived and well-merchandised stores around the country and have found three common characteristics that separate them from the rest.

#1
The merchandise selection is constantly changing in order to keep customers interested and coming into the store frequently.

By nearly every measure, the Gap is among the nation's best specialty retailers. Some experts feel it is the best retailer in any category. This lofty position is partially attributable to the fact that unlike nearly any other company in its category, the Gap stores offer fresh assortments of merchandise as often as every six weeks. Offering new merchandise that often may not be appropriate or even possible for every retailer, but there's no reason to let new or seasonal items get lost or hidden within the store. Too often this merchandise can only be found in a specific area, and if, for some reason, customers don't get into that area, they never see the newest, freshest merchandise.

Predictable departments and store layouts may be a necessity in grocery stores, but most other retailers should change their store layout constantly. This ensures each customer's shopping experience is interesting no matter how frequently the customer visits the store. It also ensures customers are exposed to as much of the merchandise as possible.

#2
Management is committed to great merchandise presentation and making sure displays are always fully stocked, neat, tidy, and organized.

There is much more to this than keeping the merchandise selection fresh and exciting. In the best-conceived and well-merchandised stores, the merchandise is beautifully displayed. All of the merchandise. All of the time.

I've been in stores where the merchandise was shopworn and tired, racks and shelves were over filled or under filled, and merchandise displays were generally unappealing. I've also visited stores where the overall look and feel of the store appeared to have been completely neglected.

Sometimes it appears the neglect has gone on for weeks or even months. When it goes on for that long, the blame falls squarely on senior management. They just don't care enough to make it a priority. But when the neglect is for only a few days or even one day, the blame falls on the people in the store—managers, assistants, and employees.

That neglected look often occurs at the end of a busy day or weekend. Store personnel tell me, "Well, we've been really busy and just haven't had time to get the store straightened up and back in shape." Do customers who come into your store late in the day deserve anything less than those who come in first thing in the morning?

For as long as I've been involved in retailing, one of the rituals has been the "hurry-up cleanup" just before visits by district managers, executives, or owners. I was standing at the counter of a store one day in earshot of the store manager who was talking on the phone. This was the part of the conversation I heard.

"Oh [expletive deleted], they're on their way? We aren't anywhere near ready yet. How long do you think it will take them to get here? We need at least another hour. I told them to get it done last night, but they got busy with customers and didn't do it. I'd better get off the phone if we're going to have half a chance of getting it done." Does this sound familiar?

While this manager's language at the counter was inappropriate in front of customers (I was one of several waiting at the cashwrap), the whole idea of making the store presentable to the company brass is a gross waste of time. If that same effort was spent keeping the store shipshape all the time, the most important people would be better served—The Customers.

There are certainly occasions when it's impossible to keep the store in pristine condition, but keeping the store neat and tidy and the merchandise well-displayed is not a once-in-a-while thing. It's an every-day, every-hour process that requires hard work and a great deal of discipline.

It's also a matter of priorities. Serving customers is always the #1 priority, but do the people in your stores know what comes second? Do they know how important it is to have fully stocked shelves? Do they know that every customer, every day is judging your store by how attractive it is, how the merchandise is displayed, and how appealing and well-maintained the shopping environment is?

Do your employees know that when they walk through the store and see something out of place, it's THEIR responsibility to take a moment and put it back where it belongs?

I've also been in stores where the process of keeping displays fresh and interesting, shelves fully stocked, and everything in pristine condition never stops. In these stores, it's part of the culture. Everyone takes great pride in making sure the store always looks ready for a visiting guest regardless of who the guest may be. Fixtures, floor coverings, and lighting to paint and wallpaper, signs, and props are all used to show off the merchandise and enhance the customers' shopping experience.

Visit one of Wynn Ferrel's Hallmark Gold Crown stores in the Kansas City, Missouri, area, and you'll see how fixtures, display cases, and signs are used to show off the merchandise in an attractive, easy-to-shop environment.

Visit Elliott's 74,000-sq.-ft. hardware store in Dallas, Texas, and you'll see how departments jam-packed with merchandise can be enhanced and items made easy to find with great signage.

Visit the sparkling St. John store in Beverly Hills, California, and you'll see how an understated, elegant color scheme can be used to make the store's designer merchandise appear to be worth every penny of its designer prices.

Visit the Nautica shop in Macy's Lennox Square store in Atlanta, Georgia, and you'll see how floors designed to look like the wooden planks on a ship's deck are used to enhance the nautical theme of the merchandise.

Visit the Paul Stuart menswear store on Chicago's famed Michigan Avenue, and you'll see how the right kind of lighting can create exactly the right mood that brings merchandise displays to life.

Visit Ken Morton, Jr.'s 7,000-sq.-ft. Haggin Oaks Golf Shop in Sacramento, California, and you'll see how signs are effectively used to identify individual suppliers' products and create eye-catching displays.

Visit the Pelican Hill Golf Shop in Newport Coast, California, and you'll see how plants and elegant furnishings such as artwork, sofas, and chairs can be used to create a comfortable, yet merchandise-focused selling environment.

#3
The best merchandisers are constantly experimenting with and fine-tuning the store layout and merchandise positioning.

From the all-important "decompression zone" in the very front of the store to the width of the aisles, everything you do to make it comfortable and convenient for the customer to enter and traverse the store is important. Merchandise placed in the front 12–15 feet of the store is often unseen and unsold because customers need a little time and space to get acclimated and get their bearings.

Widening the aisles by just a few inches can result in significant sales increases for merchandise on lower shelves. Identifying traffic bottlenecks and dead-zones within the store can help eliminate areas where sales may be lost. Attracting customers to areas within the store where traffic is light may require some research. Try installing a video camera in an inconspicuous spot, and for several days tape the traffic coming and going in poor sales areas. Viewing the tape will help you better understand what needs to be done to open the area up and attract more shoppers. (See Chapter 6 for more on video research.)

It's also important to track merchandise sales by location within the store as well as the position on display racks and shelves. A careful analysis of what's selling and in what quantity by specific location and position will provide you with information that can be used to maximize sales in every area of the store.

IT'S ABOUT BEING OBSESSIVE!

Great stores require an obsessiveness for making them look perfect all the time. "Perfect" may seem like an unattainable goal. But retailers with an obsessive approach to everything having to do with merchandising, displays, and housekeeping have a much better chance of getting close.

THE VALUE OF A CUSTOMER

arbara Johnson regularly shops in the card and gift store in her neighborhood for most of the greeting cards and wrapping paper she buys as well as some gifts. Marilyn Rafferty makes a point of stopping by her favorite clothing store at the mall about once a month to see what's new that she can add to her wardrobe. Jon and Sarah Hopkins are in the process of redecorating their home, and they like to go to their two favorite furniture stores for ideas. In recent months they've bought new living room furniture, a couple of lamps, and some other accessories. Jason and Tiffany Montrose just got married and moved into a brand new condominium. Nearly every week since moving in, they've gone shopping and have bought such things as lightbulbs, picture hangers, bed and bath linens, area rugs, and a couple of hanging plants for the patio.

DEVELOP A RELATIONSHIP

What are these retailers doing to maximize their relationships with these customers? Do they recognize how important each of these customers is to the long-term success of their businesses? Do they track how often these customers shop in their stores and how much they spend? Do they know why they've chosen their store over a competitor's? Do they know when one of these customers stops shopping in their stores and why? Do they know who their new customers are and what they'll need to do to turn them into regulars?

Barbara Johnson's favorite card and gift store would know most of these things except that the people working in the store forgot to register Barbara for the store's frequent buyer card. If they had signed her up, Barbara would be receiving cardholder benefits and the store would be able to track her purchases and market to her.

In the case of Marilyn Rafferty and her favorite clothing store, the manager and a few sales associates working there have gotten to know Marilyn, and they do everything they can to give her very special treatment. They realize how important she is to the success of the store. Unfortunately, senior management at the company doesn't place a high priority on knowing about Marilyn and others like her. They haven't done a thing to get to know and understand what makes her so valuable to the company.

They do know that customers come into the store every day. If these customers buy enough merchandise, the company will meet its numbers. But, what if customers stop coming in? Will the company know why? Will the company know what it needs to do to get those customers coming back? Will the company have instant insight into the buying tastes, interests, and habits of each of its customers?

HOW IMPORTANT
IS ONE CUSTOMER?

The two furniture stores where Jon and Sarah Hopkins shop approach the issue of knowing their customers very differently from one another. Management at Store #1 has been talking for a couple of years about adding a customer database to its computer system so the staff can track sales by individual customer. But with the new delivery trucks they had to buy, plans for a new store on the other side of town, and the trips they've had to take to the various furniture shows, management just hasn't made it a priority. They'll get around to it eventually.

Jon and Sarah have been helped at one time or another by nearly everyone who works in the store, but none of these salespeople has taken the time to start a file on them. Each salesperson gets a copy of the sales receipt for the items Jon and Sarah have purchased, but neither the company nor the salespeople have taken the time to put them all together and keep track of those purchases.

At Store #2, Cheryl Tarlow always assists Jon and Sarah. Cheryl's been to their home several times to help them decide what would best fit in with their decor. She has even delivered a couple of the smaller things they've ordered.

MAXIMIZING CUSTOMERS, NOT JUST TRANSACTIONS!

Five years ago management at Cheryl's store realized it was in the "customer" business not the "transaction" business. A new computer system with a comprehensive customer database was installed. The new system allows both management and the store's salespeople to keep track of each customer's purchases, how much they spend, what mailings and special offers they have responded to, and even how often they visit the store. The system also includes an alert feature that notifies Cheryl and the other sales associates when a regular customer hasn't been in for an extended period of time. (See Chapter 5 for more on customer databases.)

Cheryl keeps her own customer database in the portable computer she takes with her to work each day. She knows more about her customers than just about any other home furnishings salesperson in town. She keeps track of the things they already own, even those things they've bought elsewhere. Her database includes information about her customers' ages, tastes, and interests, and even the things she has shown them that they didn't buy. She also knows what they do for a living. She knows many of their birthdays and sends a birthday card every year. She even knows their children's names.

Whenever Cheryl gets something in the store that she thinks Jon and Sarah will like, she calls them, and if the item is small, she offers to bring it to their home. Whenever the store has a sale, there's always a special, invitation-only VIP event held the evening before the sale officially opens to the public. This event is for the very best customers, because the store is in the "customer" business not just the "transaction business." Over the last year, Jon and Sarah have spent three times as much in Cheryl's store as they have in Store #1.

GROWING THE RELATIONSHIP!

As young newlyweds, Jason and Tiffany are just beginning to determine which stores they like. Some of the stores they shop are the same as those their parents shop. Jason's father always buys hardware and home repair merchandise from a neighborhood hardware store—one that's part of a national buying cooperative. But Jason doesn't have the same loyalties to neighborhood stores as does his father, so he and Tiffany usually shop in stores with the biggest selection and lowest prices. A few weeks after moving into their new home, they received a letter and several discount coupons from a new home center that was about to open in their neighborhood. The letter, which was addressed directly to Jason, invited him to come in during the grand opening and take advantage of some very special merchandise offerings.

On his first visit to the store, a salesperson asked Jason whether he would like to apply for the company's credit card. Since he knew he would be buying lots of things in this kind of store, he thought a company credit card would be a good thing to have. And since the credit card also included more merchandise discounts, he signed up.

Jason received his credit card a couple of weeks later along with a welcoming letter from the company's CEO. The package contained more discount coupons; a schedule of classes on do-it-yourself home repair, remodeling, and decorating projects; and a store feedback card so he could let them know about any problems he encountered. A couple of days later Jason got a nice thank-you letter from the store manager inviting him to call any time he had a problem or needed something special.

IS YOURS A CUSTOMER-FOCUSED BUSINESS?

The customers I've profiled here are fictional, but the situations are not. At a time when retailing is more challenging and more competitive than ever, the importance of collecting information on each individual customer and using that information to manage the relationship is an absolute necessity.

One of the best views on this issue comes from William Esry, chairman and CEO of Sprint Corporation: "The globalization of commercial communication does not mean reaching customers a billion at a time. It may seem like a paradox, but global communication gives us the chance to speak intimately to each and every customer and actually have them talk back to us. In fact…the successful business of the future will know their customers by name or settle for having no customers at all."

Do you know your customers by name? Are you keeping track of what they buy and when they buy? Do you know how much they spend? Do you know what they think is important in their relationship with your store? Do you know how many customers stop doing business with your store each year? Do you know why they stop? Do you know what your customers think you do well and what you do poorly?

One of the most valuable things you can do for your business is to start building systems and procedures to answer these questions. Start today so yours isn't one of those businesses that has to settle for having "no customers at all!"

CHAPTER 5

TECHNOLOGY AS A SELLING TOOL!

S ales associates in such stores as Nordstrom have long kept "customer" books containing information about customer preferences and past purchases. Customer books can be a valuable selling tool, but there are limitations as to what you can keep track of in a physical book and how quickly you can access the information. When customer information is entered into a computerized database, on the other hand, the information is accessible to salespeople the instant a customer walks through the door. As I mentioned in the last chapter, the database can be designed to include frequency of visits and the average dollar amount spent on the last several visits. It can include a synopsis of the customer's brand and style preferences—and even the names of family members who also may be customers.

Salespeople at a hardware/home center chain can instantly pull up a history of their customers' past purchases. They then can use this information to sell the customer more of the same or to recommend something new that might better meet their needs. From the information on hand, the salesperson may suggest the customer buy a larger quantity today to save the time of an extra trip to the store. With the wide variety of merchandise available in a hardware/home center, the database also includes information on applications and how to use the products sold in the store.

ANALYZE PURCHASE HISTORY AND USE IT

At one of Southern California's better quality menswear stores, sales associates use their customer database to quickly analyze purchase history and then tailor their merchandise recommendations to the individual customer. The information they have at their fingertips allows them to show exactly the right sizes and styles for each customer. The salesperson can even recommend specific suit styles, colors, brands, fabrics, and accessories that the customer doesn't currently have in his wardrobe. For example, let's say the customer bought a sport coat on his last visit. With information on this previous purchase, the salesperson can recommend a pair of slacks or shirt that might look great with that sport coat.

A Midwest furniture store that provides decorating services includes in its database a list of major furniture items the customer already owns. After the initial visit, the decorator/salesperson posts information to the customer's database that includes styles, colors, and brands in the customer's home. When the customer next visits the store, the salesperson might say, "These lamps will go great with the color scheme in your master bedroom." Without the database, it would be difficult to keep track of this important information about every customer.

CREATIVE DATABASE APPLICATIONS

One of the best customer database applications I've found is being used by a small wine shop in northern California. The owner, a computer wizard, installed three computer terminals in his store and tied them to a very sophisticated database. While talking with a customer, the sales associate can enter the person's name in the database and instantly view purchase history.

When asked about a particular bottle of wine, the sales associate can compare it to a bottle the customer may have purchased in the past. The associate can also bring up a series of screens that provides all kinds of additional information. One screen offers reviews by wine experts and the store's other customers on a particular winery's products. Another offers suggestions on foods that are best served with this type of wine along with other serving suggestions. And still another provides word descriptions the salesperson can use to describe the taste of the wine.

After installing this sophisticated system, sales to the store's best customers doubled in the first 18 months with an overall sales increase of just under 40 percent. At a time when retail wine sales were generally flat, this small store enjoyed tremendous growth.

TECHNOLOGY AS A
TRAINING RESOURCE

Chain store operations all across the country use point-of-sale systems to provide all kinds of information to managers and sales associates. The daily report from headquarters, for example, may include information on merchandise coming into the store, sales events, the previous days sales, total sales for each sales associate, and lots of other worthwhile information. We are beginning to see these internal communication systems used to provide training and sales education information as well.

With today's satellite technology, a number of larger chains including JCPenney are using their internal systems to deliver training programs directly to the stores. What can you do if you don't have the resources of JCPenney? Among the technological tools used by smaller retailers to enhance their selling process and train their people are computer-based and Internet training programs. While most of these programs are currently limited to providing general information and basic selling skills, we are beginning to see a wide range of retail-specific online training and educational programs. The costs associated with creating such computer- and Internet-based training have come down dramatically, which is very good news for retailers.

MANUFACTURER WEB SITES

Another area where technology plays an important role in employee education is with access-code-protected manufacturer Internet sites. It's easy to see how valuable it would be if your sales associates had instant access to a manufacturer's Web site specifically designed to provide selling tips, product features and benefits, and information on competitive products. One manufacturer's Web site includes suggestions on how to sell its products along with information on accessory items and other complementary products.

Retailers who use these tools to enhance the selling process and improve the way they serve their customers have an important competitive advantage. If you haven't already taken steps to integrate these technological tools into your selling functions, I suggest you look into it.

CHAPTER
6

WHAT DO CUSTOMERS EXPERIENCE IN YOUR STORE?

D o you have a thorough understanding of your customers' actual shopping experiences in your stores? I've found that most retailers have barely scratched the surface when it comes to creating an environment that maximizes the customers' experiences in a controlled way to build sales and repeat store visits.

Focus groups and customer interviews are common research tools used in retail, but they only determine whether customers like merchandise selections, feel comfortable in the store, and are properly cared for by sales associates. This isn't enough to thoroughly understand customer shopping experiences. This type of research doesn't give a retailer enough information to make changes in store layout and design that will result in higher sales and increased customer visits.

CUSTOMER BEHAVIOR RESEARCH

Some large chains, such as Wal-Mart, Eckerd, Target, Macy's, Lowe's, and Office Depot, have used the services of Envirosell to help them gain a more thorough understanding of customer experiences in their stores. Envirosell, based in New York City, was founded by Paco Underhill, one of the nation's most insightful experts on consumer buying and author of the bestselling book *Why We Buy*. The research process Envirosell uses includes placing small video cameras in strategic positions to record customer activity as well as having researchers in the store to observe shopping activities and interview customers as they enter and exit.

The value of coupling videotape of customers shopping with the information gathered from face-to-face interviews cannot be overstated. This process provides researchers and retailers with extraordinary insight into the customers' shopping experiences—their interaction with the store, its merchandise, and the store's sales associates.

RESEARCH FOR EVERY RETAILER

If yours is a large national chain with sufficient resources to conduct this kind of research, the place to start is to contact Envirosell (www.envirosell.com). Even if you don't have the resources of a large national chain, you can still use this type of research to gain an understanding of your customers and how they shop in your stores. Begin by developing a program of customer entry and exit interviews. They have some limitations, but if you aren't already using this tool to better understand your customers and their shopping experiences, it is a good place to start.

CREATING AN ENTRY AND EXIT INTERVIEW PROGRAM

To create an effective interview program, determine exactly what information you want to gather and how you will use the information once it has been collected. You may want to find out how many of the customers who come into your store actually buy. You may want to determine how far they travel to shop in your store. You may even want some demographic information such as age range, size of family, etc.

For entry interviews, you may want to know what customers are looking for or thinking about buying when they come into your store. You may want to know if yours is the first, second, or third store they've visited; whether this is their first time in your store; or if they are regular customers.

For exit interviews, you may want to know whether the customers found what they came in to buy; whether they bought it; what they bought if they didn't find what they were looking for; and how sales associates served them. You may want to find out how long the customers were in the store, what they liked, and what they disliked. You may want to know if they plan to visit one of your competitor's stores, if they didn't find what they were looking for in yours.

I recommend you use people other than your own employees to conduct the customer interviews. You can hire temporary employees or students from a local college to do this research. A retailer in California put together a research program with the marketing department at a community college. Students conducted customer interviews at his stores using questions he and his staff had constructed. The students were, of course, paid for their time. They also received class credit for conducting the research as part of their marketing program.

Retailers operating single stores and smaller chains will find this kind of research very helpful to gain understanding and insight into customers and their shopping experiences. Once you have done this for a while, you may want to take the next step and add video to your customer research tools.

VIDEO CUSTOMER RESEARCH

There are several ways to use video as a customer research tool. For retailers with limited resources, buy the least expensive black-and-white video camera available from an industrial video supplier, install it in an unobtrusive area of the store, and connect it to a standard VHS recorder. Be sure to put the date and time on each tape.

If there is a good place to position the camera so it records your customers' actions as they go through the entire store, you will be able to observe how long customers spend time in the store, what areas of the store they visit, and whether a sales associate helped them. All of this information will help you better understand the customers' experiences in your store. Record a couple of week's worth, then sit down and take notes while you watch the tapes.

For retailers with larger stores who want to gain even more knowledge of their customers' actions, I recommend you buy or lease several small black-and-white video cameras and place them strategically throughout the store. Cameras can then be coupled to a time-lapse industrial video recorder that will record from 8 to 40 hours on a single tape. These machines automatically time- and date-stamp the recording so you can compare when customers go from one area of the store to another and how long they stay in the store.

PUTTING INTERVIEW AND VIDEO RESEARCH TOGETHER

Conducting entry and exit interviews at the same time you videotape your customers' shopping experiences is the best method I know to gain a thorough understanding and insight into how customers shop your store. By asking demographic questions in an interview and putting that information together with videotaped observations, you can learn how age, income, and other demographic factors influence how customers interact with the merchandise, your associates, and the store in general.

Video recordings also allow retailers to determine which customers visit certain departments or areas of the store and which customers get assistance from sales associates. The goal of visual merchandisers is to get customers to stop, look, touch, and buy. The only way I know to determine how often displays achieve these goals is with video. Sales data from the POS will tell you how many of the displayed items were sold during a particular period of time. But sales data can't tell you how many customers stopped and looked at the display or how many picked up an item. And it can't tell you what percentage of those customers who stopped, looked, and touched actually bought.

Video is also a great way to determine whether customers stop to read specific signs within the store or whether they pick up certain boxes or packages to read product features or other descriptive information.

THE CASHWRAP OR CHECK-OUT

Retailers can significantly benefit from observing video of customers at the cashwrap. Wouldn't it be helpful to know how long the average customer has to stand in line to buy merchandise? Wouldn't it be equally helpful to know how long they stand in line if they are the first, second, or third customer in the line? Few retailers know how many customers actually leave their stores without buying just because the checkout line is too long? And, yes, it does happen.

Recently my wife and I left a store after standing in line for several minutes. It appeared we would have to wait at least another 10 minutes before we were able to make our purchase, and we were unwilling to waste the time. And we weren't the only ones who left without buying because of the long wait.

This retailer could have used the video from this particular day along with others to determine the busiest periods of the day and then add more checkouts or schedule additional help during those peak times.

Another question that can be answered with video is how long it takes the average customer to make a purchase at the cashwrap or checkout counter once he or she gets to the front of the line. With speed and convenience as fundamental factors a customer uses to decide where to shop, retailers must do everything possible to speed up the checkout process for buyers.

After viewing the videotape, a retailer may determine that checkout is taking too long. With this information, the retailer might decide to provide additional training for cashiers to speed up the process. It might be time to make changes in the POS software or explore other operational shortcuts to provide a faster, more efficient checkout.

Other opportunities for video research might include observing merchandise pickup, repair, and return operations and procedures. Video can be used to improve every area where the customers' interaction with the store itself and with the store's associates impacts and influences their shopping experience.

TAKING CONTROL
OF CUSTOMER EXPERIENCES

We've heard a great deal about how entertainment-oriented stores are changing the way consumers shop for some kinds of merchandise. But creating a shopping environment where the customer is comfortable, the merchandise is displayed in a way that makes it easy to shop, and where the customer likes spending time may be even more important. There are plenty of stores with little or no entertainment value where customers just love to spend time.

In a shopping center not far from my home, there are two giant bookstores. One is Barnes & Noble and the other is a Crown Books Superstore. Both stores have a wide selection of books. Both provide chairs in which customers can sit comfortably while browsing and reading. Crown generally offers lower prices on bestsellers. Barnes & Noble has a Starbucks next door with an entrance into the store.

The real difference between these two stores, however, is more than just price and an adjoining Starbucks. Barnes & Noble has a far more comfortable and inviting atmosphere, and, from my less-than-scientific observations, attracts a lot more customers. As a frequent bookstore shopper, I always have trouble finding a place to park in front of Barnes & Noble. At the competing Crown store, you can always find a parking space right in front. It would be very interesting to put video cameras in both stores and see how customers react to these decidedly different shopping environments.

The research methods and tools described here will provide you with information and insights that are unavailable to you from any other source. They will provide you with an opportunity to gather information that will help you increase sales, better serve your customers, and improve the efficiency of your business.

CHAPTER 7

MAXIMIZING CUSTOMER SELLING OPPORTUNITIES!

S ince the mid-1980s, manufacturers and other industrial companies have embraced a wide range of management initiatives and strategies designed to improve operating efficiency. The common focus of such programs is how to become more competitive in the manufacturing and distribution of products.

Manufacturing high-quality products and efficiently distributing those products are key factors that allow the best companies to thrive in such a highly competitive global economy. It would be naive to think that any manufacturer could achieve 100 percent quality control or deliver customer orders on time all the time. But many of the nation's leading manufacturing companies consistently run their operations—both manufacturing and distribution—at levels of 95 percent efficiency and higher. In a purely process-oriented business, quantifying efficiency is a reasonably straightforward task. In retailing, it is more difficult, but no less important.

In the last chapter we talked about understanding customer shopping experiences. I believe retail inefficiency is most affected by how we manage customer shopping experiences. I'm not alone in thinking this way. I've talked with retailers all across the United States in virtually every retail specialty about inefficiency in stores and how it impacts their bottom line.

I'VE ASKED HUNDREDS OF RETAILERS THIS QUESTION...

Do you know what percentage of the customers who come into your stores get their questions answered correctly, are shown merchandise that meets their wants and needs, are able to find the merchandise they came in to buy, are then given every opportunity to buy it, and generally have a satisfying shopping experience?

Another way to look at it might be to ask yourself, what percentage of the "customer-selling opportunities" in our stores are being maximized? It is a complex question, but the business of selling merchandise and serving customers is complex. Consumers are faced with so many choices of places to buy that successful retailers must take extraordinary measures to get their share of the business.

The answers I get to the efficiency question run anywhere from a low of 30 percent to a high of 80 percent. The vice president of stores for a well-known specialty chain answered, "I have no idea, but it probably isn't very high, maybe 35 or 40 percent." And after talking with hundreds of retailers about their efficiency numbers, 65 percent is a pretty good place to start when looking for a retail benchmark for raising efficiency in stores.

MAXIMIZING EVERY SELLING OPPORTUNITY!

Let's assume that approximately 65 percent of the customers coming into your stores get the full treatment:

- They are warmly greeted by a sales associate.
- They get their questions answered correctly.
- They are shown the merchandise that meets their wants and needs.
- They are able to find the merchandise they came in to buy.

- They are given every opportunity to buy.
- They leave the store after having had a satisfying shopping experience.

With this fairly broad assumption, how much more volume would you do and how much more profitable would your business be if you could improve that percentage by 10 percent or even 5 percent?

Keep in mind, this is not just about how many people buy or don't buy. It is the question of maximizing every customer opportunity. Nearly every customer who goes into a supermarket or other commodity-type store buys something. So the question for these retailers isn't whether or not the customer buys but how much they buy and what steps need to be taken to make sure each customer is given the opportunity to buy some of the store's higher profit and proprietary products. For most other retail segments, determining efficiency means answering several questions and evaluating the entire shopping process.

QUESTION #1
Did the customer buy anything before leaving the store?

As every retailer knows, there is a direct correlation between how many customers come through the door each day and how many sales are made. To get customers into their stores, retailers spend tremendous amounts of money positioning their stores in high-traffic shopping malls. They spend more money creating knock-the-customers'-socks-off store environments. And they spend even more on high-profile marketing and promotional campaigns. But the ultimate question for every retailer still is, how many of the customers coming through the door each day are making purchases?

When looking for opportunities to improve overall sales efficiency, increasing the number of customers who make a purchase is a great place to start. If 50 customers come into your store each day and only 19 (38 percent) make a purchase, it's easy to see where there's room for improvement. And if 150 customers come in each day and 65 percent buy something, you still have over 50 people walking out empty handed—definitely room for improvement there, too.

QUESTION #2
If customers do buy, were they given every opportunity to buy accessories or add-on items?

This is one of the best opportunities retailers have to significantly increase sales and profits. In stores selling higher-priced merchandise, salespeople need to know how and when to present accessory or add-on items. Self-service stores should position this type of merchandise adjacent to related items. It may be necessary to position such merchandise in several places in the store. And, finally, cashiers should always mention accessories and add-ons at the cashwrap.

QUESTION #3
Do customers find everything they were looking for when they came into the store?

There are a couple of factors that influence the answer to this question. First, how easy is it to find departments and specific merchandise in your stores? It never ceases to amaze me how many stores have poor layouts and even worse signage. It makes it so much harder for customers to negotiate the store and find what they're looking for. As we continue to jam merchandise into stores and offer wider selections, it's even more important to do everything you can to make it easy for consumers to buy.

Several years ago a supermarket chain positioned a greeter at the front door of its stores. The greeter's job was to welcome customers into the store and hand out a detailed map showing where the various departments were. A good many stores have directories, but it's every bit as important to position those directories where they are most needed—when customers first enter the store. I believe even moderate-sized stores would benefit from providing customers with a detailed store layout.

The second factor influencing the customers' ability to find merchandise is the help they get from salespeople and cashiers. As a Home Depot customer, I'm always impressed when I ask a question and the sales associate actually takes me directly to the merchandise instead of saying, "It's halfway down aisle seven right across from the widgets."

QUESTION #4
Was the shopping experience convenient and pleasant enough to inspire the customer to come back and shop in our store again?

Much has been written about knock-your-socks-off entertainment-oriented stores, but a dramatic looking store isn't required to inspire customers to come back again and again. What is required is an obsessive commitment to understanding what the customer wants and expects in your kind of store and then giving them a shopping experience that's really pleasant.

MORE THAN JUST WORDS

Some restaurants have decided that we want to know our server's name and that he or she is "there to serve our needs." Is that what we really want? I was in a restaurant not long ago and "Tommy" came up to my table, smiled, identified himself as my server, and told me that he was there to make sure I got everything I needed. Tommy took my order and it was the last time I saw him. Someone else delivered the order and at the end of the meal, I had to send a search party out to find Tommy so I could get my check. I won't even go into how long it took to get through the payment process because I'm sure you know.

Customers don't want superficial, insincere service. They want, need, and expect the people helping them in stores to be attentive when they need attention. They want people working in stores to leave them alone sometimes. They want them to be available to answer questions, but they don't want them hovering. Customers want respect for themselves and their time. They want the shopping experience to be as easy and hassle-free as possible. And they want the people working in stores to be genuine and caring.

A RETAILER'S STORY

After a thorough analysis of the front-end portion of the business, which included weeks of videotaping as described in the last chapter, one 42-store chain retailer began evaluating and fine-tuning everything that impacted the customers' experiences in the stores. This process included looking at everything that influenced a customer's decision whether to buy, what to buy, and how much to buy.

The company had done some work to improve merchandise assortments, create a more attractive overall look to its stores, and fine-tune procedures so there always was enough advertised merchandise on hand. They hadn't, however, paid much attention to other factors that influenced the customers' shopping experiences including how customers came in contact with store employees. They hadn't really looked at how signage influenced what customers purchased or just how effective the signs were. They had replaced fixtures to help show off the merchandise but had never looked at how merchandise positioning within the store and on the fixtures themselves impacted sales. They had never looked at how adjacency influenced the sale of accessory and add-on merchandise.

The evaluation and analysis resulted in significant changes in how the company operated the business. The first change was a new awareness of everything that influenced the customers' experiences. Store associate and manager training programs were completely redesigned to emphasize this new way of thinking. Everyone, from store managers to sales associates to cashiers, was taught to understand how all their actions impacted customer shopping experiences. They were taught how customers were to be greeted and how the company expected every customer to be served.

Management also began to redesign store layouts and merchandise positioning so it was easier and more convenient for customers to shop the stores. Signage was improved and cashwrap counters were relocated to make checkout more convenient.

The results after the first year were quite spectacular. The percentage of customers who made a purchase increased by 14 percent. The dollar amount of the average sale increased by 8.5 percent. Along with some changes in the merchandise mix and an overall increase in sales, the company's profit margins during this period went up by two full percentage points.

HOW TO GET STARTED

Combined with the information you get from customer interviews (see Chapter 6), start counting the number of customers coming through the door every day. Determine what percentage of those customers is buying and what percentage isn't? If the percentage isn't what you think it should be, it's probably time to start your own efficiency-building initiative.

The next step is to identify why customers leave without buying. Is it hard to find things in your stores? Is signage clear and easy to read? Are departments well-defined and identified? Are accessories and add-ons placed adjacent to larger or related items? Are accessories and add-ons displayed in several places in the store? Are associates serving every customer the way you want them to be served?

These are just a few of the questions you will want to ask yourself as you go about improving efficiency in your stores. It's the place to start, and when you begin addressing the answers to these questions you will have a road map for improvement.

CHAPTER 8

WHAT EVER HAPPENED TO GREAT CUSTOMER SERVICE?

In retailing, we talk a lot about customer service and how important it is to building and maintaining a successful business. Over the past several years, most retail trade associations have embraced the notion of improving customer service and have used it as a theme for their annual meetings or conventions. Retailers representing every segment of the business have held seminars or training programs on how to improve customer service in their stores. Literally hundreds of books have been written with detailed recommendations on how to improve customer service. Yet customer service today isn't any better than when all this started.

NEWSWEEK SAID IT'S "ABYSMAL"

Every day customers get ignored. And when they are finally served, how often is it that associates not only know nothing about the merchandise, but treat the customers as though they are an intrusion? How often do you see associates chatting with each other behind the counter as customers wander around the store? How often are they talking on the phone while customers wait in line to pay for purchases?

In some retail categories, poor customer service is an accepted way of doing business. Long lines, ill-mannered and rude associates, as well as anti-customer attitudes are a common part of the everyday activities. The March 1, 2000, edition of *Newsweek* magazine described the current state of customer service in retail establishments as "abysmal." Citing a University of Michigan survey of customer satisfaction, the magazine placed much of the blame on the shortage of good workers.

It's easy to place blame on worker shortage, but the situation is much more the result of an overheated business climate that allowed for sales and profit growth in spite of worsening service. The result is that some retailers give little or no priority to customer service improvement. They actually believe customers don't care about the service they receive in stores. The thinking goes, "We haven't done anything to improve service, and customers are still buying lots of our merchandise, so they must not care." How quickly we forget!

TEN CUSTOMER SERVICE RULES

The solutions to providing great customer service are available to any retailer willing to give the issue priority. It's all there in front of us. Just think how much more business could be done if customers actually enjoyed shopping in a store. Here are 10 rules to follow every day:

1. **Warmly greet and welcome every customer into the store.**

2. **Associates should always be friendly and smile.**

3. **When a customer asks for something, associates always take them directly to the merchandise.**

4. **Train associates so they have the knowledge and ability to help customers make an informed buying decision.**

5. **Focus the store's policies, procedures, and systems on enhancing customer experiences.**

6. **Make it easy to buy.**

7. **Willingly take back merchandise customers don't like or want.**

8. **Quickly repair or replace broken merchandise.**

9. **Provide a pleasant shopping experience to every customer.**

10. **Thank customers for their business and invite them back.**

It really is a simple list of things that, when done, will ensure customers receive good service and have a pleasant experience.

WHAT IT TAKES!

To deliver the kind of service described in the list, retailers must do two things, actually it's three things. First, stop hiring ill-mannered people who really don't want to serve your customers. Sure it's hard to find good people, but when you hire someone who treats your customers poorly, it's costing you a staggering amount of lost business. I'm constantly amazed at how many people working in stores just don't like doing what they're doing and, in fact, appear to hate helping customers. And what's even more amazing to me is that someone made a conscious decision to hire these people without getting to the heart of their personalities and attitudes.

So, the second part of this is to hire nice, friendly people. This may be easier said than done, but if you staff your stores with nice, friendly people, your customers will buy more and WANT to come back again and again. In stores where associates are nice, friendly, and attentive, sales go up.

Finally, spend as much time and effort as possible teaching associates exactly how customers should be served, what they are to say, and how important every customer is to the success of the business. If yours is a large retail organization, you probably have a well-designed customer service training program that employees are required to take when they are first hired. But what happens after new hires get to the store and have been on the job a few weeks? What kind of support and ongoing training do they receive?

If yours is a smaller company, there are many kinds of public seminars and tape packages you can buy to teach your associates how to provide outstanding service. And if you can't find one that fits your needs, design your own.

EVERYDAY TRAINING!

To influence how your staff members think about their work and shape how they serve your customers, I recommend that store owners, managers, and assistants hold training sessions every day. The sessions need not be long or even formal, but they must be consistent. Talking about customer service for 10 or 15 minutes every day before the store opens or after it closes can have a dramatic impact. Short, five-minute coaching sessions with associates on the floor can also result in improved customer service. The key is to reinforce the idea that serving the store's customers in a positive and pleasant way is an essential part of everyone's job.

ARE WE MAKING PROGRESS?

When I started my consulting business back in 1987, customer service was an important topic among retailers. Today I ask you, has customer service improved, worsened, or stayed just about the same? I'd like to think it's getting better, but we still have a long way to go before it gets to where it should be and customers receive the kind of service they deserve.

CHAPTER 9

HOW STORES FARE FROM A CUSTOMER'S PERSPECTIVE

onsider this scenario: Clarice Wilson* is a 38-year-old wife and mother of three children who range in age from 9 to 14. She works part-time for a law firm in the southeastern city where she lives. She worries about her children's education and keeping them out of trouble, away from drugs, and safe from violence. She wants to make sure they grow up with the important values and skills they'll need to live rewarding lives.

Like many working homemakers, she has little time to shop for her family or for herself. Between running a busy household, working at the law office, and shuttling her children to soccer games and the like, Clarice's grocery shopping has to be done late in the evening or very early on Saturday mornings.

When she was first married back in the early 1980s, she and her friends made frequent trips to the local mall where they spent several hours shopping, eating, and enjoying each other's company. In those days, she and her friends often shopped as many as eight to 10 stores each trip. Now those social mall excursions rarely happen, and more often her mall visits are dictated by the pressing need for a particular item. Unlike in the past, she rarely has time to visit more than one or two stores.

With a higher-than-national-average household income of $75,000, she is able to dress her family fairly well; feed them well-balanced, healthy meals; and maintain an attractive, well-furnished suburban home. She and her husband are active in the community and enjoy entertaining friends.

CONVENIENCE AND VALUE

With little time to shop, Clarice is always interested in convenience and value. But they mean different things to her now than in the past. Convenience is more than location, and value is a great deal more than low prices. So, how does she decide to visit a particular store? What factors does she take into consideration before she gets in her car, drives to the store, parks, and goes in to shop?

Clarice Wilson—and millions of other consumers—isn't interested in shopping in stores that don't care about her or her specific needs. While she's considered a "nice" person by her friends, she has little tolerance for long check-out lines, rude and inattentive store employees, or taking time to go into a store and failing to find advertised merchandise in stock. In recent years, she has adopted an "I'll-never-shop-in-that-store-again" attitude when she's unable to find advertised merchandise.

WHAT DOES SHE EXPECT?

As do millions of other busy consumers, Clarice has some very specific expectations from the stores she shops.

She expects a great selection.

She doesn't have time to visit several stores to find what she wants. She's savvy enough to know the difference between a big selection of low-quality merchandise and a big selection of merchandise at various quality and price levels. She wants and expects a real choice.

She's interested in more than the lowest price.

She knows there's more to value than just low prices.

She expects to pay more for better quality merchandise, but the price must be fair. She prefers branded merchandise, but she will buy a house brand if she's convinced of its quality, durability, and value. She makes every significant buying decision based on price, value, and quality.

She expects the store to have an easy, no-hassle return policy.

In the past she bought lots of merchandise that didn't meet her needs, didn't work after she got it home, or just wasn't what she expected. Before she considers buying anything now, she wants to know about the return policy the store offers as well as product warranties.

She expects a fast, pleasant check-out.

She just doesn't have time to wait in long lines. When considering whether she will visit a particular store she has shopped in previously, she will subconsciously ask herself whether she has time. She crosses stores off her shopping list that generally have long check-out lines.

In specialty stores, she expects knowledgeable sales associates for guidance and information.

She takes pride in being an informed consumer, but sometimes must rely on sales associates to help her find the merchandise she needs. She's willing to rely on sales associates, and she's just as willing to cross off the list stores with sales associates who give her inaccurate information.

She shops in stores where she has a long-term relationship.

She is loyal to stores with sales associates who go out of their way to track down a special item in another of the company's stores. She's loyal to those stores in which she's on a first-name basis with a sales associate, the manager, or the owner. She's loyal to stores that offer her a discount or some other incentive to shop there regularly.

She's loyal to retailers who communicate with her frequently by sending a handwritten thank-you note after a purchase or a newsletter with tips and ideas, or by calling and inviting her in to see some new merchandise they know she will be interested in seeing.

She shops in stores that deliver on their advertising claims and what they promise after the sale.

When a store claims it has certain merchandise or brands, she expects to find a reasonable selection of that merchandise or brand in stock. When special ordering an item, she expects it to be in when promised. When merchandise is to be delivered to her home, she expects it to be delivered on time and by competent and friendly delivery people. And she wants a prompt, efficient resolution when there's a problem.

She expects the individuals working in the stores to be attentive, pleasant, and professional.

It would be nice if they were friendly as well, but she'll settle for the first three. She leads a hectic life, and she's still nice to the people with whom she comes in contact, so she expects the people working in stores to treat her the same way.

She is loyal to stores that deliver on their promises.

She has a clear idea of the kinds of stores she wants to shop, and she's intensely loyal when she finds one. She will always shop there first. When she's looking for new furniture, apparel, gifts, and household items, she always goes to the store in which she has had the best experience in the past. And she nearly always goes to those stores with the intention of buying on that visit.

She refers her friends and acquaintances to those stores that do the best job of meeting her wants, needs, and expectations.

She is proud of her decisions to shop in certain stores.

She knows she's a consumer with high expectations and shares information about specific stores with her friends.

SHE'S NOT UNUSUAL

Clarice Johnson is not unusual in what she wants and expects from the stores she shops. She is very much like millions of other American women who lead busy lives taking care of their families and managing a career. Although she doesn't feel comfortable buying online, she does use her home computer to gather information on products and stores.

By some estimates more than 70 percent of the consumer dollars spent in the United States is controlled by women. With more than half of those women active in the work force, retailers must continually search for ways to better serve these powerful consumers.

What are you doing to make sure Clarice Johnson and others like her become loyal customers and return to shop in your store again and again?

*Clarice Johnson is a fictional character who is a composite of the characteristics of many female shoppers.

SALESPEOPLE FROM A CUSTOMER'S PERSPECTIVE

The best retail salespeople stand out from others in their stores because of their own strong personal motivation, a burning desire to succeed, well-defined personal and professional goals, and the ability to get the job done. They have exceptional sales and communication skills, and they exhibit an extraordinary level of professionalism as they sell to and serve their customers. They are the best.

What do customers say about the best retail salespeople? What do they think separates the best from the rest?

"They always make me feel welcome in the store, with a warm smile and friendly greeting."

The best retail sales associates walk up to every single customer, smile warmly, and offer a friendly greeting laying the groundwork for making a sale. I am constantly amazed at how few people working in retail stores understand the importance of making the customer feel welcome and wanted in the store. With all the talk about the importance of customer service (see Chapter 8), there are still front-line employees who either blandly greet customers with no warmth and enthusiasm or don't greet them at all. And there are others who still walk up with that blank expression and chirp, "Can I help you?"

"They always make me feel at ease."

The best retail sales associates make every customer feel at ease, regardless of the surroundings or the circumstances. There are lots of stores in which customers just don't feel comfortable. They may be intimidated by the merchandise or the surroundings. For example, a good many men are very uncomfortable going into a lingerie store or department to buy a gift. An effective lingerie salesperson does everything possible to put a male customer at ease in this "uncomfortable" environment.

"They are always professional in how they conduct themselves."

While it may not be possible to describe professionalism in exact terms, customers certainly know it when they see it. From appearance to demeanor to attitude, the best sales associates are always professional in their work.

"They always ask just the right questions and show me exactly the right merchandise."

Recently several studies have tried to determine what consumers want and expect in their dealings with retail employees. Here are three of the most common complaints consumers tell researchers:

1. I can't get answers to questions about the merchandise.

2. Individuals working in stores do little to help me understand the merchandise.

3. Individuals working in stores spend little time or effort determining what I want or need.

"They answer all my questions even though they may seem unimportant or senseless to them."

It's easy to see why a sales associate might get bored answering the same question over and over again or answering questions that seem stupid or irrelevant. But sales associates should realize how important it is for every customer to feel comfortable with his or her buying decision. The best associates are patient and understanding, and they answer every question in a way that does not insult the customer or make the customer feel as though the question is foolish.

"They always make me feel confident that my relationship with them and with the store won't end after I've made a purchase."

Savvy salespeople understand they are in the relationship business. They have their own personal customer book with the names, phone numbers, addresses, and purchasing history of their best customers. They frequently call or drop customers a note telling them about new merchandise they are sure the customer will be interested in buying. When merchandise must be special ordered, they keep customers apprised of the progress including when customers can expect delivery of their orders. (See Chapter 4 for more on the value of a customer.)

"They always make me feel like I've made a good decision about what I've bought."

A good many customers don't need a salesperson to tell them they've made a good decision. But just as many have trouble making buying decisions and sometimes are unsure they are buying just the right merchandise to meet their specific wants and needs. The best sales associates can recognize those customers who need this kind of decision-making support and encouragement, and they give it to them.

"They know everything about the merchandise that's available for sale in the store."

In a marketplace filled with look-alike merchandise, the best salespeople know everything about what they have in their stores and what makes it different from or better than other merchandise. The very best also know exactly what merchandise is being sold by their major competitors and how their store's merchandise will better suit the customers' wants and needs. Just as they are sales and service experts, the very best retail salespeople are also merchandise experts. (See more on making salespeople experts in Chapter 11.)

"They know everything about their store's policies and procedures."

Watching the best retail salespeople work is like watching any master of a profession. They are able to help every customer through the buying process because they know exactly what has to be done and how to get things done efficiently. They respect a customer's time before, during, and after the sale. By having a thorough understanding of the store's policies and procedures, they are better able to serve customers.

"They treat me like I'm special."

Customers don't buy on logic alone. They often buy from a particular salesperson just because they like that person. It's a simple concept that seems to be lost on some salespeople. Not on the best. They know if they treat every customer like the special person they are, they will sell more merchandise.

"They let me know how much they appreciate my business."

The best retail salespeople let their customers know how much they appreciate their business with handwritten thank-you notes and follow-up telephone calls. They do more than just sell merchandise. They give their customers ideas and insights into how they can use the merchandise, how to get the most out of their purchases, and how to maintain their purchases so they receive lasting satisfaction.

DO THESE PEOPLE EXIST? ABSOLUTELY!

The very best retail sales associates are the people who lead the sales floor month after month. They are the best because they always do the things that not only create delighted customers but create delighted management as well. Do these people exist? Absolutely!

They work in stores where there are great opportunities. They work in stores where they are respected and appreciated. And they work in stores where management is committed to helping them improve and grow as people.

◆

THE EVERYDAY BUSINESS OF SELLING

Taking more control of the selling process begins with teaching your sales associates exactly how you want your customers served. This is the quickest way to increase sales and maximize profits in your stores. When you teach sales associates everything you can about the merchandise and make them experts, you can justify higher prices, and you will have a better chance of creating long-term relationships with your customers as well.

◆

WHAT IS YOUR SELLING STRATEGY?

Self-service and minimum-service stores, in nearly every merchandise category, have enjoyed great popularity with consumers. Part of the initial appeal was the belief that minimal or self-service stores sold the same merchandise as their full-service counterparts at lower prices. While that may have been true in the early days, it certainly is not the situation today.

In the current retail environment, minimal and self-service retailers often must depend on lower quality, close-out, discontinued, or private-label and mass-produced merchandise to justify their pricing and generate sufficient profits.

Consumers want to know...

• Will I get the right merchandise to meet my specific needs?

• If I buy a video recorder or DVD player at a store without well-trained sales associates, will I get a machine with the features I really want?

• If I'm going out to buy a new suit and visit a self-service-type store with racks of clothes and little or no help, will I be able to select a suit that fits me properly?

• If I buy a new power saw from a warehouse store where the only help I get is from the cashier who rings up my sale, will I get the right model for my needs?

Retailers want to know...

• Are we maximizing our profits on the merchandise we sell?

• Are we maximizing each customer by making sure they are given every opportunity to buy?

• If I have well-trained, highly-skilled sales associates serving our customers, will I distinguish my store from the competition?

Time pressures continue to force consumers to make quicker buying decisions with less information. A more focused, customer-oriented selling strategy can be an extremely effective way to stand out from the competition and build long-term relationships with time-pressed consumers.

Here's a lesson learned by successful Internet merchants: If they give prospective customers as much information as possible, they significantly increase the likelihood of repeat sales. What Internet merchants don't have is the ability to develop face-to-face personal relationships with their customers.

IS IT TIME FOR A
NEW SELLING STRATEGY?

Over the years, attractive stores and a great selection have helped specialty retailers stand out in a crowded marketplace. Improving customer service has become a competitive edge as well. A small but growing number of retailers that sell popularly priced merchandise have begun to adopt a selling strategy that previously was found only in stores selling luxury goods. That strategy is built around well-trained, professional sales associates.

In stores where this strategy works best, sales associates have a clearly defined job.

- They make the customer feel welcome and comfortable.

- They get to know everything about a customer's tastes, wants, needs, and expectations.

- They show the appropriate merchandise.

- They provide the customer with as much information as needed to make an informed buying decision.

- They give every customer an opportunity to buy.

This at first may seem much like the way merchandise was sold in the days before giant discount stores and self-service ruled the marketplace, but there are some very distinct differences.

A SELLING STRATEGY BUILT ON KNOWLEDGE!

A selling strategy built on knowledge means immersing sales associates in comprehensive, ongoing product training programs designed to make them experts in their categories. Individual specialty stores and chains selling everything from home decorating accessories to jewelry to golf equipment have used this approach as a means to stand out from every other store in the community.

Some Examples...

At one regional jewelry chain, sales associates are so knowledgeable that the company's stores have been recognized by consumers as "The Best Place to Shop." The customers see the value of buying jewelry from real experts on gold, silver, platinum, diamonds, and other precious stones.

Prior to the spring gardening season for each of the last two years, the owner of a small chain of garden centers put her employees through a series of educational seminars on lawn care, growing a vegetable garden, and how to plant and care for a wide variety of flowers. The program was built around those vegetables, flowers, and plants that were best suited to the geographic area. Employees also learned about lawn mowers, hedge trimmers, and other gardening equipment sold in the stores.

At a three-store hardware chain, sales associates spend two days every month learning about the merchandise and a third day learning how to do various home repair, remodeling, and decorating projects. When a customer comes into one of their stores to buy the items needed to install a garbage disposal, sales associates know exactly what questions to ask. They know what specific items the customer will need to complete the project, and they can provide some guidance on how to deal with any problems that may arise.

A COSTLY APPROACH!

Yes, it takes a good deal of time and effort to turn sales associates into experts. But it's well worth the investment. The jewelry chain I mentioned increased its average sale per customer by 18 percent in one year. The garden center owner saw a 25 percent increase in sales the first season and 35 percent the second.

The hardware retailer has not only increased his average sale per customer but also his total sales have grown by more than 15 percent for each of the three years he has offered sales training. During that same three-year period, a competing home center chain opened a store a few blocks away. After an initial drop in business, customers began coming back to the hardware retailer because they couldn't find anyone in the home center who could give them the help they needed.

THE LEARNING PROCESS

In larger retail organizations, the foundation for this knowledge and skill building usually takes place in a training room. For smaller ones, learning and skill building happens in the store, often on the selling floor. This is more difficult, but not impossible.

For every retailer it takes commitment, dedication, and resources. Teach your sales associates these things and your customers will notice—they will buy more and they will buy exactly the right merchandise. Your suppliers will notice, because you will sell more. Your sales associates will be more productive and feel better about their jobs. And your company will be more successful.

Who could ask for more?

CHAPTER 12

IS SALESMANSHIP A VANISHING SKILL?

How often do customers leave your store without buying because of some action or inaction by a sales associate? If yours is a full-service retail business with sales associates who are expected to help customers select the right merchandise for their needs and you answered the above question, "often" or even "sometimes," then finding a solution to this problem can pay tremendous dividends.

Sales performance is usually measured and evaluated by sales volume, gross profit, or margin percentage, but rarely by examining closing ratios, average sale dollar amounts, numbers of units sold, or whether the sale is made to a repeat customer. Some of these may be difficult to measure, but they can provide another method for evaluating sales performance. They also can provide a great deal of insight into the kind of job your sales associates are really doing.

WATCH OUT FOR THESE RED FLAGS

1. A sales associate who talks with twice as many customers as other associates and closes half as many sales.

2. A sales associate who only talks with a few customers each week and sells mostly advertised merchandise.

3. A sales associate who only sells the primary item (and no accessories) to most customers.

4. A sales associate who sells only his or her favorite brands, colors, models, or styles rather than giving customers the opportunity to buy from the store's entire inventory.

5. A sales associate who finds it easier to present and sell only lower- and moderately priced merchandise and who completely avoids high-ticket items.

6. A sales associate who puts out just enough effort to

achieve average earnings and does only enough work to stay in the middle of the pack.

7. A sales associate who almost never gets requested by a repeat customer.

8. A sales associate who makes no effort to keep informed about the newest merchandise or how to present and sell that merchandise.

WHAT THEY'RE COMFORTABLE SELLING

In my consulting work, I've had the opportunity to interview hundreds of sales associates across the country. Two of the questions I've asked are: How do you decide what merchandise to present to a customer? Why do you like to sell certain brands, styles, or models over others in your store?

I've found that most sales associates present essentially the same brands, styles, or models to every customer who shows an interest in a particular type of merchandise. The customer may ask to see a particular brand. But given the opportunity, the sales associate will show one or two other models as well. They show what they are comfortable selling, what they know the most about, or models they prefer for themselves.

Your sales associates often are the dominant influence over what merchandise gets shown and sold to your customers. Making a sale, of course, is the first priority, but sales associates don't always understand or look at the complete picture with respect to stocking and selling each merchandise category, brand, or individual item in your store.

IMPROVING SALES PERFORMANCE

The process of shaping, influencing, and guiding sales performance should be an integral part of your entire merchandise/sales strategy. Here are some important ingredients to include when developing an effective sales performance improvement plan.

#1
Establish sales performance standards.

While hourly, weekly, and monthly sales totals are the most common gauge for measuring individual results, they don't mean much if a salesperson talks with a hundred customers but actually sells only a small percentage.

By establishing sales performance standards, you can determine exactly what is expected in the way of closing percentages; sales volume in specific product categories; and any of a broad range of sales, profit, and merchandise measurement categories. For example, a shoe store company analyzing the sales performance of its best salespeople might look at these specifics. Top performers talk with an average of 22 customers each day and sell 61 percent of those customers at least one pair of shoes. They sell 19 percent of their customers two pairs of shoes. And they sell 12 percent three pairs. The analysis also shows they sell shoe trees, socks, belts, and other accessories to an average of 33 percent of the customers daily.

Analyzing and evaluating the performance of your best sales associates will help you develop tangible sales performance standards that can then be used as a benchmark for the entire sales staff. Keep in mind that no matter how you establish standards of performance, those standards must be tailored to fit individual stores and individual sales-people. Performance standards may be influenced by the number of hours and days worked by sales associates along with intangible factors such as their level of experience and amount of training. Performance standards can increase sales performance effectively or demoralize associates if you fail to communicate standards properly and gear them to each associate.

Whatever criteria you use to establish sales performance standards, it is imperative to make sure they are fair, clearly communicated, frequently reviewed, strictly adhered to, and used as a means to build and improve the overall perform-ance of your sales staff.

#2
Make it so!

You can't wish performance improvement. Managers must constantly communicate with their sales associates about performance standards and give them a clear idea of what is expected.

One of the most effective store managers I know conducts a brief, informal meeting with his salespeople every day. He reviews what happened in the store the day before—what sales were made and what merchandise was sold. He verbally pats people on the back with positive reinforcement. He gently chastises those individuals who performed below par the previous day. He encourages all his associates to focus on what they are doing and avoid distractions from the daily task of selling and providing every single customer with a positive and rewarding shopping experience.

In the simplest of terms, he's shaping and improving the performance of his salespeople by talking with them and by placing a high priority on what they sell, how they sell it, and how they perform their jobs—every single day.

Ask yourself this question, is there anything else your store managers do each day that's more important or has more potential for producing significant sales increases than having a well-planned daily meeting with the sales staff? Your managers can provide the guidance, encouragement, and tools sales associates need to do the job better. How about getting your store managers started today?

No other method will do a better job of communicating these ideas and information. Memos and company newsletters inform, but they can't coach, counsel, prod, encourage, or direct your sales staff as well as the store manager who meets and talks with them every single day.

Even mass-merchants and discount stores have found that daily meetings help their hourly associates stay focused on providing friendly, courteous service. A 15-minute daily meeting can keep associates excited and motivated during the busiest times of the year.

#3
Rewards!

One of the most interesting things I've learned in my interviews with retail salespeople is how they feel about the rewards they get for their selling efforts. Salespeople who are not among the store's top performers often place a great deal of importance on commissions or spiffs.

This is not to say financial rewards are not important to top performers as well, but they are often better able to understand the intangible rewards that come from being very good at serving the needs of customers. These include the praise and positive reinforcement they get from management. But it's also the self-satisfaction they feel from having a large base of customers who ask for them upon entering the store and who refer their friends and acquaintances.

Managers must communicate the value of these intangibles to the entire sales staff. If they are conducted properly, performance evaluations can be effective tools to accomplish this.

#4
Evaluation!

Over the last several years, some companies have eliminated the annual performance review. They've learned that once a year isn't enough when the goal is to shape and improve performance. In these organizations the annual performance review process had become the most hated time of the year, and the negatives outweighed any positives.

If real performance improvement is to take place, evaluations must be done frequently—no less than once a month. And the focus should be on the goal of improving performance, not simply listing things an associate did right or wrong.

The most effective sales performance evaluations focus on how the sales associate went about achieving the previous month's sales totals. The manager can walk the salesperson through the month discussing various customers, what they bought, and what could have been done to sell more. The manager also can talk with the salesperson about those customers who didn't buy, why they didn't buy, and how the customer could have been dealt with more effectively.

The evaluation process may also include a discussion on what the manager can do to help the salesperson achieve his or her sales goals next month.

DRIVING PERFORMANCE!

What your sales associates say and how they deal with your customers shouldn't be left to chance. With thorough planning and effective execution, you can influence, shape, and control the sales process to ensure what you want to sell gets sold and your customers are served the way you want them served.

◆

GREAT STORE MANAGERS MAKE GREAT STORES!

T o succeed in today's highly competitive marketplace, retail businesses must get extraordinary effort from everyone in the company. They must always try to hire people with a burning desire to be successful. And they must employ the most talented people they can possibly find in every position. This is especially true when it comes to the position of store manager.

In every area of retailing—from supermarkets to specialty

◆

stores—the most successful organizations share the common characteristic of having talented, dedicated store managers.

A consulting client of mine found himself in a perplexing situation. One of his stores had everything going for it—a terrific location, lots of foot traffic, great neighboring stores, and a huge population of mid- to upper-income-level consumers living within a few blocks. Exactly what was needed to be successful in his segment of retail.

The problem? The store just wasn't achieving the sales volume it was capable of generating. Neither the CEO nor I was quite sure why. Other stores in the chain were doing much better even without all the built-in advantages of this store. There was one difference. The other stores had really good managers. The manager in this store was reasonably competent, but definitely not outstanding, so my client replaced him.

Almost immediately things began to change. Soon the store was not only meeting its sales goals but also exceeding them. At last the store was living up to its expectations. Hiring the right manager turned an underachieving store into a top performer.

GREAT STORES NEED GREAT MANAGERS! MEDIOCRE STORES THAT ASPIRE TO BE GREAT ALSO NEED GREAT MANAGERS!

No matter how big or small the company, the success of any retail business depends upon what happens in the store;

and a skilled, dedicated, and talented manager makes good things happen in a store. The store manager has a great deal of control over the attitude, tempo, feeling, and, ultimately, the success of the store.

- Store managers who become satisfied with themselves make self-satisfied stores!

- Dull store managers make dull stores!

- Fearful store managers make fearful stores!

- Arrogant store managers make arrogant stores!

- Mediocre store managers make mediocre stores!

- Customer-focused store managers make customer-focused stores!

- Committed store managers make committed stores!

- Adventurous store managers make adventurous stores!

- Great store managers make great stores!

The challenge in retailing today is how to go about identifying, finding, hiring, and keeping talented store managers.

CREATING A PROFILE

The first step, and one that is sometimes overlooked, is to develop a written profile of what you want in a store manager. This is done by defining in very specific terms the skills, attributes, attitudes, knowledge, and experience the person must have to be a successful store manager in your company. This is a critical part of the process. Without completing this important step, the entire hiring process is little more than a guessing game. How can you find the perfect person if you don't know what kind of person you're looking for?

Do you have the very best, most talented, and most qualified people managing your stores? If not, why not? For your retail business to achieve great success, you must have great managers. If you can't find qualified people who are already great managers, it is absolutely necessary to start teaching the people you already have to be great managers.

I realize there are a good many retail businesses that have enjoyed considerable success by making their stores "manager proof." They've created policies, procedures, systems, and processes that allow almost anyone with minimal skills and talent to run the store. But even in these organizations, there are store managers who are able to get more from their people and do whatever is necessary to outperform the other stores in the chain.

Most retail businesses still rely on their store managers to guide, shape, and control the destiny of their stores and no matter which retail organization I look at, I find stores that consistently outperform the rest. There are a few great performing stores that generate high sales volume simply because they are in the right location or because of some other geographic or demographic reason. But the stores I'm addressing here are the ones that consistently outperform average stores. Stores that set the standard for everyone else to follow. Great stores are able to achieve extraordinary sales levels because they are run by great managers!

Once you have a model for who and what you want, you can go about looking for candidates who fit your model or you can begin taking steps to train and develop the people you already have working for you. Some characteristics found in great managers, however, can't be developed; they are a fundamental part of the person's character.

WHAT IS A GREAT STORE MANAGER?

While not a totally comprehensive list, here are 10 of the most common skills, attributes, attitudes, and characteristics I've found among great store managers I've met and talked with in my work. Some of these great managers have come from single-store operations. Others have been employed by large national chains. The great ones have all been hard working, talented, dedicated people who get things done and know how to make things happen.

#1
Great store managers are
highly effective communicators.

This is the most fundamental and valuable of all store management skills. One glaring difference between mediocre managers and great ones is that great ones are able to articulate exactly what they want and expect from their people. Great store managers are able not only to get people to do the tasks around the store, but get people to want to do the tasks. Great store managers are also good listeners. After all, half of communication is listening. Without effective communication skills, it is impossible to be a great store manager.

#2
Great store managers inspire trust and build confidence.

Leadership means setting an example. Great store managers are confident and self-assured. Through their own actions they inspire trust and confidence in the people around them. They are not arrogant or braggarts; instead they know and understand their own capabilities and use that knowledge to inspire their people. Without the ability to inspire trust and build confidence, it is impossible to be an effective leader, and the best store managers are also great leaders.

#3
Great store managers are never completely satisfied.

Great store managers have an insatiable need for constant improvement. They enjoy accomplishing things and reaching goals, but soon afterward look for new challenges. Great store managers often are more satisfied accomplishing the task itself rather than with the results obtained by doing so. In my travels

I visit a lot of stores. I can almost always tell what kind of manager is running a store by spending some time wandering around, looking at displays, talking with employees, and watching them deal with customers. Stores run by great managers always seem to look a little better, have a better "feeling," and the employees are more upbeat and positive.

#4
Great store managers are highly competitive.

This is another of the fundamental characteristics of great leaders, and it doesn't seem to make much difference whether they are male or female, young or old. They want to be among the best, and they're willing to make the effort and inspire their people to do whatever it takes to get there. Great store managers are never satisfied with mediocrity. They look at the success of their store as a personal challenge and constantly tinker with it and fine-tune things to get just a little more out of it.

#5
Great store managers have high expectations.

They expect a lot from their people. They expect them to work harder than others. They expect them to do the job better. They expect them to do whatever it takes to achieve the store's goals. Great store managers know their people have the capacity and ability to do more than they are doing. Great store managers are able to raise performance levels with higher expectations. They also have high expectations for themselves.

#6
Great store managers delegate authority and responsibility.

This is one of those characteristics that really separates great ones from the rest. Great managers are confident enough in their people not only to delegate authority for the task but responsibility for the results as well. To effectively delegate authority and responsibility, great managers must also be great teachers. They make sure their people have the knowledge and skills needed to do the job. They delegate then get out of the way.

#7
Great store managers are organized and detail oriented.

In many retail organizations there are store managers who are able to achieve high sales numbers, but who fail to do a good job of keeping track of all the details that are part of running the store. They are great sales managers but not great store managers. Great store managers are able to do both. Their recordkeeping is meticulous. Their inventory count is accurate. Their reports are timely, thorough, and clear. Their paperwork is up to date.

#8
Great store managers have a sense of urgency.

Great store managers don't procrastinate. They get things done when they need to get done. They understand that a great store opens every single day with a new set of challenges and problems. They can't waste time dealing with yesterday's, so they solve today's problems today. They understand their job is to satisfy the needs and demands of customers, employees, and the company. Things just can't be put off until tomorrow.

#9
Great store managers are problem solvers.

By some estimates, managers in high-volume stores spend as much as 50 percent of their time solving problems and putting out fires. Great store managers are also great at satisfying a dissatisfied customer, smoothing out problems between employees, and making sure everyone is happy. They are diplomatic, patient, and able to see things from both sides of a situation.

#10
Great store managers
are sales driven.

The measurement of success in any retail business is how much merchandise is sold and how profitably. Great stores are always judged by this criteria, and great store managers are judged by this same criteria. They know that to generate lots of sales they must have a great looking store; a staff of dedicated, talented, hard-working people; the right merchandise selection; lots of satisfied customers; and an obsession with keeping operating costs in line.

DO THESE PEOPLE ACTUALLY EXIST?

Now, before the skeptics say, "That doesn't sound like any of my managers," I want you to step back and take a very close look at your managers and compare how they stack up to this list. They may not be a perfect match, but I'll bet if your business is successful, you've got a couple of store managers who come pretty close.

One of the best store managers who ever worked for me had nearly all of these characteristics except one. He was absolutely awful when it came to keeping up with reports and paperwork. So, I made sure he had the very best assistant I could find.

It's easy to see when you look at these skills, attributes, attitudes, and characteristics that these are very special people. If you have some of them working for you, make sure you let them know how much you appreciate their hard work and dedication. After all, another retailer may be out there looking to snatch them away.

◆

CHAPTER 14

FROM MANAGEMENT TO LEADERSHIP

Retail managers today must be highly-effective leaders. Managing requires talent, knowledge, and some very important skills. But effective leadership also requires some personal characteristics and attributes that are not easily taught. Someone with a reasonable amount of talent, a desire to learn and grow, and a willingness to work hard and commit himself or herself to the job of managing a store can become an effective manager. But the store

◆

manager who can inspire people to achieve extraordinary performance—and executives or owners who are most successful—are almost always different. They possess personal characteristics that help them accomplish what others in the same set of circumstances are unable to accomplish.

WHAT IS A LEADER?

If we look at the history of the world, it's easy to list the great political and military leaders. Even in retailing, it's easy enough to name some great leaders. Retailers such as J.C. Penney, John G. McCrory, and Gen. Robert Wood, the visionary who led Sears in the early days of their retail growth, each had a significant impact on the industry. In every sense they were true leaders.

In recent years, such leaders as Les Wexner of The Limited; H. Wayne Huizenga, founder of Blockbuster Video; Gordon Segal of Crate & Barrel; and Wal-Mart's Sam Walton have led their companies to extraordinary growth and success.

Not all great leaders become famous in the process. For example, there's a woman in a suburb of Phoenix, Arizona, who manages a fast-food restaurant with a staff of 65 mostly part-time employees. Her store generates several million dollars in business each year and is among the best-performing stores in the chain.

If you were to ask the individuals working in that store what it's like to work for her, they would go on and on about what a wonderful person she is, how great she is to work for, and how they would do almost anything for her. They would tell you how she constantly challenges them to work harder and do a better job, how she praises them for the little things they do, and how she always lets them know about changes in the company's products or policies. They would tell you that when things get really busy, she'll ask them what they want her to do to help out and then she'll work right alongside them well past the time she would be expected to go home to her family. They'd tell you how she always encourages them to do their best and that she approaches everything she does with an excited and enthusiastic attitude— every single day.

Is she more than a manager? Yes.
Is she an effective leader? Definitely.

If you were to talk to the executives in her company, they would tell you employee turnover in her store is the lowest in the chain, shrink numbers are the lowest, and she stays right on target with her operating budget month after month, year after year.

NOT JUST POWER

While we often see powerful, outspoken, visionary people in positions of leadership, it's not always the case. For many years leadership was associated with power. People who had a great deal of power and wielded that power with authority were looked upon as great leaders.

In today's business climate, the people with the most power are not necessarily the most effective leaders. Some of the most effective leaders are unassuming, soft-spoken people who understand that getting things done and achieving outstanding performance can be accomplished without resorting to the use of power or control.

Effective leaders often possess a vision of how they want their organizations to function and the goals they want to achieve. In the case of a store manager, the vision may be someone else's or even that of a group of people. But it's the store manager's responsibility to make that vision of success become a reality. And that takes leadership. One of the best definitions of leadership comes from author Vance Packard.

"Leadership appears to be the art of getting others to want to do something that you are convinced should be done."

The most effective store leaders are those who get other people to see what needs to be accomplished, to want to work hard, and to do whatever it takes to achieve their goals and objectives. Easy to say, tougher to do.

YOU CAN'T DO IT ALONE!

The attitude "If you want something done right, you have to do it yourself" is an all-too-common roadblock to achieving great success. Successful store leaders surround themselves with the best people they can find, teach those people everything they can about how to do the job, and give them every opportunity to succeed.

The most effective leaders are nearly always the best teachers and coaches. Whether it's one-on-one or in a group, effective leaders constantly teach and coach their staff. They give positive, constructive feedback; keep the staff apprised of what it will take to get things done; and continue to raise performance expectation levels.

Some of the most effective store leaders I've known are also great cheerleaders. They celebrate great performance by starting store meetings with applause, or having everyone cheer for the individuals who achieve the highest levels of performance. They give all sorts of rewards when people do something special, and they even hold one-day contests with prizes and awards.

A lot of business people think these kinds of things are a little corny. But in my experience, overall performance and employee morale is higher in stores where celebration and performance rewards are a way of life, as opposed to stores where the manager takes a no-fun, hard-line management approach.

MODELING LEADERSHIP

Anyone who has ever had the responsibility of parenting knows that the most powerful influences over a child's actions are the things parents, siblings, and peers say and do every day. Those same powerful influences are prevalent in the workplace.

Store managers who moan and groan about corporate policies; look for short-cuts; are rude; or who don't provide customers with friendly, responsive service can expect their employees to do the same. Store leaders who approach their jobs with enthusiasm; always talk about the company, store, merchandise, and customers in a positive way; and do everything they can to improve and grow have a much better chance of getting their people to follow suit.

I have put together a list of characteristics for effective leaders. Leaders most often are:

Ambitious	Forward-looking
Broad-minded	Honest
Caring	Imaginative
Competent	Independent
Cooperative	Intelligent
Courageous	Inspiring
Dependable	Mature
Determined	Self-confident
Enthusiastic	Self-controlled
Fair-minded	Straightforward

Do these characteristics describe your store managers? If not, how can you transform your store managers into leaders?

MAKING SURE YOUR MANAGERS ARE LEADERS

Begin by taking a close look at the assistants working in your stores or anyone else who's on track to be considered for store leadership. Do they have any of the characteristics I've listed?

If your store leader prospects don't have these attributes, then you may find it worthwhile to reevaluate your hiring efforts so you start looking for these characteristics in prospective employees. You will also find it useful to evaluate everything you are doing to develop managers-leaders and identify the best ways to help your people develop and enhance these leadership characteristics.

Some people will never be great leaders no matter what you do to help them. Many of these characteristics begin to develop early in life and become enhanced as the person matures.

Also, it's important to keep in mind these characteristics are not necessarily age-specific. Many young people can become great leaders if they receive the right opportunities, guidance, and coaching. You must work to recognize leadership characteristics and make every effort to help these prospective leaders live up to their potential.

CHAPTER 15

EXPLORE THE POSSIBILITIES: WHAT IF...?

I n the seminar I conduct on leadership for retail managers, I ask participants this question: On a scale of one to 10, with one as poor and 10 as excellent, how would you rate your own personal creativity? I don't mean artistic creativity. I mean opening one's mind and exploring alternative, more creative methods and opportunities for selling more merchandise, growing and managing the business, and leading people.

When I first began asking this question, I was somewhat puzzled by the number of store managers who rated themselves only between three and six. The feeling of not being particularly creative isn't unusual for managers in highly structured chain-store operations, but conservative, personal creativity evaluations seem to be equally prevalent in a broad cross section of retail companies without regard to size. Store managers don't think of their jobs as creative endeavors, and often they don't think of themselves as creative people.

If you own, operate, or manage a retail business, you are probably more creative than you think. And in today's challenging environment, it would benefit you to work on those creative skills. Creativity can be nurtured and encouraged. It can be developed as well. But, if you don't use your own creativity to look for opportunities or explore solutions to problems, you can't take advantage of one of your most powerful management and leadership tools.

When confronted with a problem or unique situation, most of us rely on past experiences or what we've seen others do in similar situations. We find that it's easier to rely on tried-and-true methods rather than explore new solutions. Are we getting the best results from this "business-as-usual" approach? Before I go any further, let me clarify a couple of things. I'm not a proponent of the "touchy-feely" school of management. I believe an effective leader must have a wide variety of skills and abilities including those usually considered "soft" skills, but I don't believe in an ethereal approach to leadership.

I believe in practical, usable, tangible methods for operating a business successfully. By thinking creatively, you will be better able to solve problems, and likely will find managing your business and leading your people more rewarding as well.

If you study the most effective leaders in any field, you will find most of them are pragmatic, no-nonsense people who are able to clearly define their roles and take the steps necessary to move the business forward. Most have open minds, and they encourage everyone in their organizations to explore alternative solutions to the challenges they face each day.

THE "WHAT-IF" QUESTION

You can begin the process of creative development by asking yourself and others around you: WHAT IF we tried this? Or, WHAT IF we did it another way? The WHAT-IF question is the jumping off point for exploring creative answers and solutions. It won't instantly make you and your staff more creative, but it will get everyone to start looking for and exploring creative answers and solutions to business problems and opportunities.

Is the WHAT-IF question an integral part of the problem-solving process in your organization? Does the WHAT-IF question enable you to start looking for new opportunities and exploring new ways to do things? Here are some examples of what I mean by WHAT-IF thinking.

CHALLENGE: HOW TO DRAMATICALLY INCREASE ACCESSORY AND ADD-ON SALES

In every merchandise category, maximizing accessory and add-on sales will increase profits. Most retailers use traditional methods to increase sales of accessory and add-on merchandise, but let's take a look at some unconventional solutions.

1. TRADITIONAL APPROACH: Create strategically placed, eye-catching accessory and add-on merchandise displays near the check-out counter or in other high-traffic areas.

WHAT IF a women's apparel retailer hangs tags on shirts, sweaters, and other tops with a photograph of the item along with a coordinating skirt, belt, pair of shoes, or piece of fashion jewelry?

WHAT IF a hardware/home center has a display right in the middle of the paint department showing everything a do-it-yourselfer needs to paint a room including paint, brushes, rollers, roller pan, masking tape, a tip sheet for doing the job, and anything else the customer might need?

WHAT IF a luggage retailer creates a one-page sheet listing basic travel accessories and arranges for local travel agents to include the accessory sheet with airline tickets and travel itineraries? What if the sheet also includes overseas travel tips that describe how to use certain accessories?

WHAT IF a sporting goods store creates displays in

hard goods departments (golf, weightlifting, skiing, bicycling, etc.) that show mannequins wearing complete apparel outfits along with the appropriate accessories for that particular sport? What if the display is priced as a complete outfit?

2. TRADITIONAL APPROACH: Teach employees how to suggestion-sell accessory and add-on merchandise.

WHAT IF employees are taught that every customer must be given an opportunity to buy appropriate accessory and add-on merchandise?

WHAT IF cashiers in stores that sell portable, battery-operated items are taught to ask every customer if they need batteries?

WHAT IF delivery people for appliance and furniture stores carry a selection of accessory merchandise in their trucks and give every customer the opportunity to buy those items?

WHAT IF customers who buy higher-ticket merchandise receive by mail a catalog of accessories and add-on merchandise a few days after their initial purchase—and are encouraged to call or come back within a certain period of time to buy those items at a special reduced price?

3. TRADITIONAL APPROACH: Offer financial incentives to encourage employees to sell accessory and add-on merchandise.

WHAT IF a portion of sales associate performance evaluations is based on how many customers buy accessory and add-on merchandise?

WHAT IF a portion of sales associate performance evaluations is based on how many multiple-item sales are made during the month?

WHAT IF in those stores where higher-ticket merchandise is sold, sales associates call previous customers and tell them about new accessory and add-on items for use with their original purchases?

4. TRADITIONAL APPROACH: Offer special pricing to encourage customers to buy accessory and add-on merchandise.

WHAT IF customers who buy an item that requires additional purchases (i.e., batteries or film) receive a frequent-buyer card that the sales associate or cashier punches for each purchase, and after 10 or 20 purchases, they get something free?

WHAT IF in a menswear store new customers receive an "Accessory Club" card entitling them to a rebate or other incentive for every $300 in ties, belts, socks, and other accessories they purchase?

WHAT IF instead of a discount, every customer who buys a complete sporting goods package, apparel outfit, set of luggage, paint-a-room package, etc., has their name entered into a drawing for an in-store gift certificate, tickets to a major sporting event or concert, or another desirable incentive?

CHALLENGE: HOW TO MAKE EVERY CUSTOMER FEEL WANTED AND WELCOME IN YOUR STORES EVERY DAY

TRADITIONAL APPROACH: Conduct customer service training classes and teach associates the value and importance of offering friendly service.

WHAT IF you make it a company policy to only hire nice people who are outgoing, friendly, and genuinely care about people?

WHAT IF every employee smiles and says hello to every customer they pass no matter where the employee is in the store or what else they are doing?

WHAT IF employees are encouraged to walk customers to the front door of the store as they leave, and even help carry their purchases to their cars?

WHAT IF customers receive a handwritten thank-you note after they make a purchase? This happens in Nordstrom and a few other stores, but what if it's done in hardware stores, sporting goods stores, luggage stores, paint stores, gourmet food stores, bookstores, or even golf shops?

WHAT IF store managers spend an hour or so each day as a greeter at the front door welcoming customers as they come in, making sure they are able to find what they want, and thank them for their business as they leave?

WHAT IF the store owner, senior-level executives, and store managers call 15–20 customers each week and ask them about their experiences in the store? Was their shopping experience pleasant and satisfying? Were staff members friendly and helpful?

CHALLENGE: BAD LOCATION

You have a store located in a financially depressed area with high unemployment and little prospect for improving conditions in the near future.

TRADITIONAL APPROACH: Cut overhead, layoff employees, ride out the storm, or close the business.

WHAT IF you get all the merchants in the area together and begin sharing mailing lists, conducting joint promotions and events, and building a committed group of retailers who are willing to do what's necessary to turn the community around and create opportunities for everyone?

WHAT IF there is a way to raise funds, either from within the community or from outside, to attract new businesses, clean up an unsightly building, or begin promoting the community as a shopping destination?

WHAT IF some little-known state or federal funding programs could help in your efforts?

IS WHAT-IF THINKING A MAGIC PILL?

WHAT-IF thinking won't produce magic results without a few other steps. Most ideas generated by creative thinking aren't instantly ready for implementation. They may require some research, further study and refinement, and maybe even some testing. But, WHAT-IF thinking will open the door. How successful you are at using WHAT-IF thinking will depend on what you do to put the ideas that come from this creative process into action.

CHAPTER 16

PLANNING AND PROFILING TO HEAD OFF TURNOVER

How much will employee turnover cost your company this year? Some of the costs are not always obvious or easy to track. Let's say I'm the owner of Whalin's Hardware. Over the last year I hired a total of 28 new employees. Eight of them are still employed at my store today along with the six who have worked in the store for several years.

How much did it cost me to hire these new people, train

them to do the job, and pay their salaries and benefits? By most estimates the hard costs associated with recruiting, hiring, and initially training a new, part-time retail employee is at least $1,500 or a total of $30,000 lost for the 20 employees who didn't stay. These are the obvious costs.

What about the sales we lost because these new employees didn't know how to sell accessories and add-on merchandise? What about the sales we lost because these new employees weren't able to find what the customer needed? And what about the time the store manager and I spent coaching and training the new employees?

What about the time we spent trying to correct wrong SKU numbers that were entered into the POS terminal? And what about the amount of merchandise and cash we may have lost from employee theft? Calculate salaries and benefits for the weeks until a new employee became productive, and you have a very costly part of doing business. Added together, these hidden costs are even greater than the initial $1,500 we spent getting the new person hired in the first place.

Hiring the wrong person is a costly and often unnecessary burden on your business. Losing good people to the competition is even more costly and often just as unnecessary.

THE HIRING STRATEGY!

Some retail organizations hire as many people as possible, let them seek their own level of performance, and weed out those who don't make the grade. In other companies the entire hiring process, new employee training and orientation, and the guidance of new employees during the critical first few weeks is left in the hands of managers who are already overloaded with responsibilities. The usual result is the wrong people are hired, they get little in the way of training or orientation, and receive almost no direction in the first few weeks of employment.

It's no wonder employee turnover is so high in organizations using these two approaches. What is surprising is that high employee turnover is sometimes a problem in what are otherwise well-run companies.

THE VERY BEST PLACE TO WORK

Retail businesses with low employee turnover do two things better than the others. First, they have a clearly defined idea of what kinds of people will do well working in certain kinds of jobs. And second, they understand the absolute priority of creating a workplace where people want to work (see Chapter 18).

The ideal way to ensure you have lots of qualified applicants is to create the kind of workplace that will earn a reputation within the community as the very best place to work. Retailers who have the reputation as the place where people "want" to work have been able to attract more than enough qualified applicants to keep their stores staffed with good people.

STRATEGIC MANAGEMENT DECISIONS

Doing what it takes to hire the right people in the first place and then create the kind of place where top-notch employees want to stay and work for a long time are both strategic management decisions. In my experience, senior executives and owners in organizations with excessive employee turnover frequently don't know how much the problem is costing their companies.

If this is the situation in your business, let me suggest you take some time to do the research outlined below.

1. Determine exactly how many people were working in your company on the last day of last year.

2. Determine how many W-2s your company sent out at the end of the year.

3. Subtract the total number of people employed at the end of the year from the total number of W-2s, and you will know approximately how many people left your company within the last year.

4. Now take that number and multiply it by $1,800 (the average cost of finding, hiring, and training a new employee). You will then have a better picture of the hard costs associated with employee turnover.

5. Add your own estimate of the other costs associated with recruiting, interviewing, training, and getting new employees up to a reasonable level of performance. If you have several people involved in the recruitment and hiring of new employees (personnel department, district/regional managers, department managers, etc.), make sure you estimate their time as well.

Once you gather all this data, you will have a much better understanding of just how much employee turnover is costing your company. Every well-run retail business constantly looks for ways to eliminate waste, cut unnecessary costs, and operate more efficiently. Excessive employee turnover is one of those areas in which you can make some real headway by using a different approach.

HIRING THE RIGHT PEOPLE!

Before you run an ad, set up interviews, or do anything else, create a detailed profile of the kind of person you want working in your store and serving your customers. As described in Chapter 13 on store managers, profiling is important for every position.

You want to know—What do they think? How do they act? What kind of personality do they have? What are their priorities in life? How do they dress? Do they have personal goals? What are their accomplishments? What are their skills, attitudes, standards, and values?

Defining these last four characteristics may become the most valuable part of the profiling process. By clearly defining the specific skills, attitudes, standards, and values the ideal candidate should have, you will have a much clearer picture of the people you want working in your stores. Knowing who you are looking for will significantly increase the chances of finding and hiring those people. Determining skills can be done during the interview and with good pre-employment tests. It is more difficult to determine attitudes, standards, and values, but that doesn't mean you shouldn't try. An effective interview and the right pre-employment tests can help determine these characteristics as well.

THE PROFILING PROCESS!

The key here is to clearly and in as much detail as possible define the person you want to hire in your stores before you start looking for that person. Getting as many people as possible involved in the profiling process will help create a clearer profile. In larger organizations, get input from people in all levels of the company. In smaller companies, you might want to create the profile yourself and then show it to acquaintances you have from other businesses to see if they have any suggestions. Profiling job candidates has been successfully used in many other industries for some time now. A non-retail point of view can be helpful.

Take a look back at the people who have come and gone from your stores in a short period of time. Comparing them to your profile, you probably will find that these people and the job didn't match. There are all kinds of reasons people leave, and further examination of some of these reasons may help you refine your profile.

REASONS PEOPLE LEAVE

- The work wasn't what the person expected.
- The person couldn't do the job the way you wanted it done.
- The person wasn't suited for retail.
- The person didn't like the hours.
- The person lacked the social skills to serve customers.
- The person was quiet and shy around people—your customers.
- The person didn't like working for a male manager, or the person didn't like working for a female manager.
- The person wasn't able to fit into the company or store culture.

Even if you've spent years in retail and believe you have all the tools you need to hire the right people, you'll find creating a written profile is one of the best things you'll ever do to help ensure you build a great workforce. While you won't completely avoid mismatches, creating a profile will dramatically increase your odds of hiring the right person.

Good interviewing skills, well-constructed pre-employment tests, and even your own knowledge and intuition are not enough. With the high cost of employee turnover, everything you do to eliminate hiring mistakes and hire the most qualified candidates will pay real dividends.

SIX TIPS FOR HIRING BETTER FRONT-LINE EMPLOYEES

Here are six cost-effective steps you can take—beginning today—that will help you attract the best, most qualified, prospective employees, get them hired, and help them become part of the store team.

#1
Run employment ads designed to attract the best candidates!

Whether you have one store or a thousand, attracting the most qualified job applicants is a marketing job. Most employment ads are written to screen out anyone who may not be qualified rather than attract those people who are most qualified. It is a backward approach to any marketing effort.

This may seem like a subtle difference, but think about the goals of any marketing message—get the attention of anyone who might be interested and give that person a compelling reason to take action. The most effective employment ads have the same goal. They grab the attention of the most qualified candidates and give them compelling reasons to pick up the phone and call or come in to fill out an application.

Employment ads that accomplish the goal of attracting qualified applicants start with an attention-grabbing headline—a headline that is geared toward the wants and needs of front-line employees. They also include lots of compelling reasons for the qualified applicant to work in your stores. Again, those reasons must focus on what's important to front-line employees.

In other words, why should they want to work in your store? Remember, it's about *their* wants and needs—not yours. And we know that such things as flexible work schedules, better-than-average pay, and an interesting, challenging place to work are all things that attract people to jobs.

#2
Recruit everywhere!

Signs in store windows and newspaper classifieds aren't the only ways to attract the best applicants. In fact, they may be the least effective. As you visit restaurants and other businesses, keep a look out for friendly, pleasant people who might be ideal candidates to work in your store.

And retailers should be doing everything they can to recruit young people to retailing from colleges and high schools. Contrary to the way America's young people have been portrayed in the media over the years, most young workers will do what you ask of them, and they can make a real contribution to the success of your business.

#3
Put your best foot forward!

Whether it's in your ads, during the interview, or while conducting pre-employment screening, everyone responsible for these activities needs to understand the recruiting process and present a positive image of the company.

Some time ago I was talking with one of my clients in his office. Across the hall, one of his managers was conducting a pre-employment interview. Every few minutes this manager would answer a phone call or talk with another employee who would stick his head through the door to ask a question. During one of the phone calls, she started yelling at the person on the other end of the line, and near the end of the interview when an employee stuck her head in to ask a question, the manager proceeded to yell and berate her in front of the applicant. What kind of impression do you suppose all this made on the prospective employee?

#4
Conduct thorough interviews!

Here's where a good many companies get into trouble. Human resource or personnel departments may be conducting pre-employment interviews in some operations, but the interviewing process in most retail businesses is still in the hands of store managers. Although it is time-consuming and difficult, interviewing is still one of the best ways to ensure you get the right people. But there are no shortcuts. At one large regional chain, the average pre-employment interview lasts eight minutes. What chance do you think a manager has of actually getting to know anything about an applicant in such a short time? An effective pre-employment interview should take at the very least 45 minutes. The goal is to get enough information about the person sitting in front of you to make an informed hiring decision. In 45 minutes to an hour, the interviewer can ask the right kinds of questions and get the information needed to determine whether the applicant fits the profile you have for the position and will become a productive member of the store team. It is a daunting task. It takes patience and a great deal of concentration.

Interviewing is a skill that can be taught and developed. If you are the owner of or senior executive with a company and you haven't invested the time to teach your managers the interview skills they need to hire the best candidates, you are leaving the process to chance. Skilled, trained interviewers know how to put an applicant at ease. They know what questions to ask and when to ask them. By quickly gaining insight into the applicant and what he or she thinks and believes, a skilled interviewer can gather the information needed to make a better hiring decision.

#5
Give every applicant a chance!

A study conducted by the Robert Half organization found that more than 75 percent of the time those individuals interviewed at the end of the interview cycle got the job rather that those at the beginning. Most interviewers fail to take thorough notes and tend to hire the people who are most recently on their minds. Does this mean the people interviewed early in the process are any less qualified?

In addition, interviewers often decide whether they will even consider hiring the applicant way too early in the process. Certainly there are applicants who don't have the social skills needed to serve customers, but making the decision too soon might mean you don't get past an applicant's nervousness or even basic shyness. You may have some very good candidates who haven't the skills needed to present themselves well in an interview but who may still make excellent employees.

#6
Hire nice, hardworking people with positive attitudes!

Hiring nice, hardworking people with positive attitudes definitely should be part of your profile. You can teach new employees many things, but you can't teach them to be nice or have a positive attitude. These attributes must be part of who the new employees already are. How much business is lost because employees are rude or simply don't care about serving the store's customers? It is impossible to measure.

◆

CHAPTER 17

WHAT ARE YOU DOING TO MOTIVATE YOUR EMPLOYEES?

The things retailers must do to improve performance and encourage employees to feel good about the company and their work have changed a great deal in the last several years. It wasn't long ago that managers relied on the "fear factor" as their sole means for motivating employees. The fear of losing one's job was so prevalent in some retail organizations that employees sometimes quit on their own just to stay ahead of the axe. And, of course, the

◆

constant fear of losing one's job did little for morale. Today, managers embrace a wide variety of tools to shape how front-line employees work and how they feel about their jobs.

There's a wonderful quote by Jan Carlzon, former Scandinavian Airlines CEO and the bestselling author of *Moments of Truth,* that addresses both fear and love as motivational tools. "There are two great motivators in life. One is fear. The other is love. You can manage by fear, but you will ensure that people don't perform up to their real capabilities. But if you manage people by love—that is, if you show them respect and trust—they perform up to their real capabilities. They dare to take risks. They even make mistakes. Nothing can hurt."

GROUP AND INDIVIDUAL INCENTIVE PROGRAMS

The challenge is how to effectively balance costly benefit and incentive programs with the front-line managers' abilities and skills to create a positive, motivational work environment. A growing number of retailers are re-evaluating the way they use financial rewards to motivate their people. While Nordstrom and other department stores have had success with fairly traditional commission systems, there are a good many retailers that use group incentives to accomplish their sales and service goals.

Sandy Sardella, the owner of Pismo Contemporary Art Glass and Pismo Contemporary Art Furniture in Denver, Colorado, puts a percentage of the store's total sales each month in an incentive pool for employees. The pool is then divided up with full-time employees receiving an equal share and part-time employees receiving a lesser share.

Incentive pools and other group-based programs accomplish several goals. They help eliminate the battle over whose customer it is and whether it's "my turn" or "your turn." They also help create a team approach to serving customers. And one of the most significant benefits is that employees no longer have to be coerced into doing the other tasks like restocking and cleaning up around the store. Group incentives help employees understand how everything they do contributes to the store's success. Incentive pools and group incentives may not be appropriate or even workable for every retail business. But they can be a great way to get everyone working together to achieve common goals.

Retailers selling high-ticket items create some of the most innovative individual incentive programs. A good number of well-known consumer electronics, furniture, and such other high-ticket retailers no longer use traditional percentage-of-sales commission programs. Instead they use contests that award merchandise and prizes, trips, celebrations, parties, and even paid days off to motivate their employees and create excitement in their stores.

KEY CONSIDERATIONS WHEN CREATING AN INCENTIVE OR REWARD PROGRAM

To accomplish the goal of motivating employees to sell more and work harder, there are some things to keep in mind.

- Incentives must be of great value to the participants.

- Programs must be changed frequently to keep participants interested.

- Rules must always be fair to everyone involved.

Financial incentives alone are not enough. Managers must have good people skills and be excellent communicators to encourage every employee to work up to his or her potential.

If you can give front-line retail employees the same level of respect and trust usually reserved for the company's managers and executives, they will work harder, be more loyal, and approach their work with a great deal more passion and enthusiasm. You might find it useful to ask the upper echelon in your organization whether they deal differently with each other than with front-line employees.

UNDERSTANDING THE DIFFERENCES

To create a motivational climate where everyone receives the same level of respect and trust, you must understand the differences in the way people look at their jobs. For professionals, the results of their work are often tangible, measurable, and, when done well, highly motivational.

District or territory managers receive their evaluations and often their pay based on sales or other tangible results of the stores they manage. When they see the financial rewards of their work, it is often enough to motivate them to work even harder.

For hourly, front-line employees, the pay itself usually isn't enough to provide much motivation. It takes something more. Commissioned retail salespeople, particularly those who have been earning their living selling for some time, may look upon themselves as entrepreneurs. They may think they work for themselves and don't need management to motivate them to work harder. This is particularly true with commissioned retail salespeople who have enjoyed some success.

Managers who understand that everyone needs encouragement, direction, recognition of good work, and a clear understanding of what is expected of them are able to get the best from every type of employee.

LITTLE THINGS HAVE THE MOST IMPACT ON SHAPING EMPLOYEE PERFORMANCE

- Savvy managers make sure they praise an employee's performance in front of others or in store meetings where it has the most impact.

- Savvy managers send handwritten thank-you notes to employees who go above and beyond what's expected or who do exemplary work.

• Savvy managers keep everyone informed as quickly as possible whenever significant changes occur in the organization or within the store. This accomplishes two goals. It makes everyone feel as though they're a part of the team and it helps quash some of the rumors that invariably start any time there are significant changes.

• Savvy managers are sensitive to their employees' personal and family problems.

• Savvy managers understand that no matter how harried or busy they are, they won't be successful without the hard work, cooperation, and dedication of their employees.

• Savvy managers understand that people are individuals and not everyone responds to the same things. Some employees need lots of direction and guidance, others need little. Some employees need frequent feedback on their performance, others need it only occasionally.

• Savvy managers don't get so close to their employees that they lose objectivity when evaluating performance.

• Savvy managers understand that to maximize a store's performance, everyone must work in harmony. People have good and bad days. The most effective managers are sensitive to the moods of their people and how they impact the store every single day. Some days the manager must be a cheerleader, other days a counselor, and still others a taskmaster.

• Savvy managers keep everyone focused on the task of serving customer needs. They keep disruptions to a minimum, and any time those disruptions occur, they quickly refocus everyone back on serving customers.

• Savvy managers understand they are part of the store team. They pull their weight, participate in tasks that allow them to work alongside employees, and share the experiences of both success and failure with their employees.

CHAPTER
18

DO PEOPLE REALLY WANT TO WORK IN YOUR STORE?

W ith the ongoing debate over raising the minimum wage, one fact sometimes gets overlooked: What are the real reasons people work where they work? Is it solely for the money?

I was in a music store in my neighborhood talking with one of the employees about new CDs from artists we both liked. Since I'm always on the lookout for insights into what's happening in stores, I began to guide the conversation around to how he liked his job. I asked him how long he had worked in the store. He said he'd been with the company for eight years and in that store for five. I said, "That seems like quite a long time, you must like it here." Prior to my making that comment, he had been somewhat passive. At that point he got very excited and animated in his gestures. "I love this job!" he exclaimed. "Where else can I be around music that I love, work with my friends here in the store, dress almost any way I want, and get paid besides?"

WHAT PEOPLE LIKE ABOUT THEIR JOBS

#1
They like companies and managers who pay attention to them.

Nearly every store owner, retail executive, and manager I meet is busy—very busy—sometimes too busy to talk with or pay attention to their salespeople. If you want to create the kind of workplace where good people thrive, management must pay attention to and spend time talking with the employees.

#2
They like companies and managers who recognize and appreciate their work.

Appreciation is among the most effective management

tools of all. Sincere appreciation can be given either verbally or as part of a special program designed to recognize exceptional performance. Both are important.

#3
They like working for managers who genuinely care about them.

Here is an idea that can pay tremendous dividends to an organization. Make one of the criteria for hiring or promoting managers their ability and desire to relate to, get close to, and support their staff. Some store managers are able to get extraordinary performance from ordinary individuals because the employees are devoted to them.

#4
They like to have fun.

No, you won't find this in most management books. But creating a store environment where management, employees, and even customers are encouraged to laugh, have fun, and enjoy themselves often results in higher sales numbers. I don't mean to let things get out of control, but create the kind of workplace where everyone is relaxed and comfortable enough to enjoy the business of serving customers. How often have you been in a store where everyone has a grim look on their face and is taking everything too seriously? Not exactly the kind of place where customers want to buy or employees want to work. Maybe it's time to loosen up a little and have some fun.

#5
They like to know they are contributing to the success of the business.

One of the newest, most widely acclaimed management concepts is open-book management. Open-book management encourages everyone to look at themselves as contributors and partners in the company's success rather than as employees. This revolutionary management concept has helped some companies redefine their businesses. It allows everyone in the company to participate actively in achieving financial goals.

If your employees don't really enjoy working in your stores, maybe it's time to look for some ways to make your stores the kind of place people really do want to work.

◆

CHAPTER 19

GET MAXIMUM IMPACT FROM YOUR ADVERTISING DOLLARS!

Advertising effectiveness is one of those issues that never goes away. Retailers constantly try to determine whether consumers find their advertising compelling enough to come in and buy. For larger retail companies, determining what's working and what's not is very difficult if not impossible. Within a few days or weeks, a major department store might run full-page newspaper ads, put inserts in the Sunday paper, send out a direct-mail piece,

◆

and run a series of TV spots. With such a barrage, it's difficult to determine what's enticing customers. For small- and mid-sized retailers who generally use a more focused media mix, determining what works and what doesn't is somewhat easier.

No matter who you are or where you advertise, it always seems to come back to the famous quote by John Wanamaker, the Philadelphia department store merchant. Way back in the early part of the 1900s, he said, "I know half of my advertising dollars are wasted, I just don't know which half." Here we are in the 21st century with sophisticated technology and evaluation methods at our disposal, and we still can't figure out where our advertising dollars are best spent.

THE RIGHT SOMEONE AND THE RIGHT MEDIA!

The challenge is more complex than ever before. Retailers need to know a great deal more than just whether their advertising is selling merchandise. They need to know if they're reaching the right audience. With just a couple additional words, the old AT&T advertising theme "Reach Out and Touch Someone" might be appropriate for retail advertisers. Today retailers are trying to make sure their advertising dollars "Reach Out and Touch the RIGHT Someone!"

HOW COMPELLING IS YOUR ADVERTISING MESSAGE?

For many years, advertising copywriter Gary Halbert conducted seminars around the country for direct marketers. When talking about how to write advertising copy, he would get everyone thinking about making the message compelling by presenting the following scenario. Participants were to imagine they were opening a hamburger stand in direct competition with the one Gary was opening across the street. He asked them to tell him what they would offer as a competitive advantage for their stand over his.

Invariably, participants mentioned the same competitive advantages—the best meat, lower prices, the freshest buns, great service, an easy-to-see sign, and sometimes even the best people. Gary would tell his audiences they could have all those advantages. The only thing he wanted was—a starving crowd!

For retail advertising copy to be effective, the words, pictures, and graphics must create that starving crowd. A compelling advertising message generates a hunger for the merchandise and for the store itself. Too many retailers focus their advertising solely on reduced prices to attract customers. While a low price certainly can be compelling, it isn't the only way to get customers through the door. It's easy to write an advertising message proclaiming low prices, but today, with so many retailers claiming *they* have the lowest prices, will the customer believe you?

USING HUMAN EMOTIONS

Creating an advertising message built on compelling human emotions is more difficult. This kind of advertising uses words and pictures to appeal to the prospective customer's desire to have the merchandise. An effective advertising message may compel prospective customers to come into your store to buy a new Rolex watch so they can be the envy of their friends. An effective advertising message may compel prospective customers to come into your store for a card or gift for their mothers because they feel guilty for being too busy to visit.

An effective advertising message may compel customers to visit your store to buy the newest toys and clothes for their children. Maybe the buyers didn't have such nice clothes or toys when they were young. They made a promise to themselves to make sure their children always had the best of everything. Coming into your store will help them keep that promise—if your advertising message is right.

It is nearly impossible to watch the television commercials produced by Hallmark Cards without feeling some emotion. The message is designed to touch our hearts and make us want to visit a Hallmark store, buy a card, and let the people we care about know how we feel. The Hallmark folks are masters at understanding the value of a compelling message.

But this kind of an emotional message may not be appropriate for your business. There are all kinds of human emotions and desires that will compel customers to come into your store. I'm always surprised how many retail ads don't tell customers how easy it is to do business with them. Compelling reasons might include convenient hours or locations, extended payment options, delivery, or any number of other convenience-oriented factors that are important to time-starved consumers.

EVERY WORD MUST COUNT!

Throughout his long career, advertising genius David Ogilvey stressed the importance of making every word in the advertisement count. "The copy must be human and very simple, keyed right down to its market," he said. "Concrete figures must be substituted for atmospheric claims, clichés must give way to facts, and empty exhortations to alluring offers."

Pick up a magazine or newspaper, watch a TV commercial, or listen to the radio, and you will invariably find ads that are filled with "atmospheric claims and clichés" without so much as an inkling of an alluring offer. These ads simply aren't believable and probably don't do much good.

You might find this exercise enlightening. Go back and read your store's advertising copy from last year. If you use radio and TV, read the scripts. Read every print ad. Ask yourself, does every word count? Are we making atmospheric claims or do we spell out the legitimate differences between our stores and those of our competitors? And, finally, does the copy compel prospective customers to want to come in and buy?

USING THE RIGHT MEDIA TO REACH THE RIGHT CUSTOMERS!

Recently, I met with the general manager of a small chain of toy stores. I'll refer to her as Marjorie. Since the first of the year, she had been running a series of small display ads in a local magazine geared toward parents. This was the first time she had used the magazine and made the decision to advertise in this publication because it reached her target audience. Since the ads started running, several of Marjorie's regular customers mentioned them, but she had no real data on how effective they were at generating sales.

At the same time, she was doing some direct mail to her in-house mailing list. During the last 12 months she had tried some small ads in the local daily newspaper. In addition to the mailings, magazine, and newspaper ads, her company usually ran a limited schedule of TV spots during the last two months of the year. How can she identify what's working and what's not?

It would be easy to look at overall sales results and say, "If they're up, the advertising is working. If they're down, it's not." But we all know, it isn't that simple. There are always a number of factors that impact a store's sales. The weather, merchandise selection, store personnel, competitive climate, and a host of other things can affect sales.

One of my favorite ways to determine advertising effectiveness is to do a media test. For print media, the best way is to offer special merchandise that is only promoted in that publication. You can also run a coupon with an offer that's only available to readers of that publication. You'll be amazed at how helpful this kind of testing is at determining the effectiveness of a particular publication.

You can test radio or television stations with special merchandise offers as well, although it's a little more difficult to determine results. For some kinds of stores, unique merchandise offers and even free-with-purchase offers can be used to test radio and television advertising. The key is to require customers to identify where they heard about it in order to get the special offer.

A sporting goods retailer tested the effectiveness of radio stations in his area by advertising a free package of sports socks with every athletic shoe purchase. He aired ads with this offer on one radio station. To get the free socks the customer had to mention the radio station offer. Three weeks later the retailer aired the same ad on a competing radio station. He then compared the results and began running a regular series of ads on the winning station.

THE RIGHT MEDIA

Deciding which media will have the most impact and produce the most sales for you depends upon a wide range of factors. What will work best depends upon:

- The kind of stores you operate.

- The merchandise.

- The competitive environment within the local media.

- The competitive environment within the retail marketplace.

- The image you want to create for your store.

- How you want to be positioned in the marketplace.

- The demographic makeup of the community.

- The time of year.

- The customers you want to reach.

DAILY NEWSPAPERS

For more than 100 years, daily newspapers have wrapped their editorial content with advertising from retailers. With the decline in newspaper readership over the last several years, the retailer/newspaper relationship has become strained. Studies show that fewer consumers read daily papers and those who do spend less time each day doing so.

I've heard some great newspaper advertising success stories from retailers in rural areas. With a small circulation, rural newspapers usually can provide retailers with larger display ads at lower costs than their big-city counterparts. The decision to advertise in daily newspapers should be based on a variety of things. As a general rule, if you want to reach consumers over age 50, newspapers will do a tremendous job accomplishing that goal. But, if you're trying to deliver your message to consumers under age 35, you will likely have more success with other advertising methods.

SUNDAY INSERTS

I advise small retailers to stay out of newspapers unless their budget will allow them to buy display ads of at least a quarter-page in size. This same advice applies to Sunday inserts. It's also important to keep in mind that if you can't afford to do a first-rate job producing the insert and you can't do them several times a year, don't waste your money.

Often, Sunday newspaper inserts deliver great results, but not always. Since some Sunday newspapers include as many as 20–30 inserts, it is absolutely essential to prepare an eye-catching design, write compelling copy, and use quality photography to present the merchandise.

You can do some targeting with display ads by placing your ad in a specific section of the paper. Most large-circulation newspapers enable you to place your insert in targeted geographic areas or even by ZIP Code. Targeting your advertising message to those consumers who are most likely to shop in your stores will improve the results.

WEEKLY SHOPPERS AND PENNYSAVERS

It's easy to knock weekly shoppers and pennysavers since these kinds of newspapers are free in news racks or sometimes thrown in people's driveways. They are usually poorly produced with ads all jumbled together, awful looking graphics, and bad quality photos. But advertising in them is very inexpensive, and every time I do a retail marketing seminar, someone in the audience invariably tells me how successful these publications have been for his or her store.

For some kinds of stores, weekly shoppers work, as they reach nearly every household in the community, and often bargain-hunting consumers read them. If you think they may work for you, here are some things to remember. First, your ad is likely to get lost from time to time in the clutter of hundreds of other ads, so it's best to run it every week for at least a couple of months. Second, be certain to move the placement of your ad on the page every week or two. And third, use coupons. Cost-conscious, bargain-hunting consumers love coupons.

MAGAZINES

While usually more costly than daily newspapers, specialty consumer magazines allow you to target a specific group of consumers who are interested in the kind of merchandise you sell. Local and regional home and garden magazines provide a great opportunity for home and garden retailers. Parenting magazines provide a great opportunity for children's apparel, educational toys, children's furniture, and a broad range of other retailers who want to reach this audience. If you're trying to reach a teenage or young adult audience, nearly every community has one or more music and entertainment-oriented magazine that may be the ideal vehicle.

YELLOW PAGES

Every home in the country has at least one book of *Yellow Pages*. And nearly every retailer has agonized over whether they should be in the *Yellow Pages* at all. If you sell merchandise or services that consumers can order without seeing, need on an emergency basis, or can buy without visiting the store, you will probably benefit from an ad in the *Yellow Pages*.

There are really only two kinds of ads to place—a single line listing or the biggest ad on the page. If you sell flowers, repair services, or anything else that fits into the above criteria, make sure your ad is the first one consumers see when they look in your category. If you run a display ad that's too small, it is unlikely you will get the call, so make it big.

Also, don't make the mistake of running other kinds of ads and telling consumers to see your ad in the *Yellow Pages*. After all, you aren't the only retailer with an ad there, and consumers will see all your competitors' ads as well.

DIRECT MAIL

I strongly believe in the value of direct mail. Retailers of every kind—from large national chains to single-store merchants—have had tremendous success with direct-mail advertising campaigns. You can target your message to exactly the customer you want to reach. You can mail to your own customer list or to every household in the community. You can measure and evaluate response and results. You can use a tremendous variety of vehicles to deliver your message—from postcards and letters to catalogs, self-mailers, and posters. You can even use an audio- or videotape to deliver your message. And you can deliver a detailed message because you aren't limited by time or space.

Targeted direct mail should not be confused with junk mail. Junk mailers often use Third-Class postage to deliver their message to a mass audience. The most successful retail direct-mail campaigns use a highly targeted approach and deliver their message to consumers who are most likely to buy from their stores. With the right list and the right message delivered at the right time, direct mail is one of the most effective advertising methods retailers have at their disposal.

RADIO

Radio, like direct mail, is among the most effective ways for retailers to advertise. With the wide diversity of radio stations in most large markets, retailers can do a great job of targeting their message. Unlike the decline of newspaper readership, the number of people listening to the radio has increased every year for the past 10 years.

What I like most about radio is that an advertiser can create intimacy with the listener by using an announcer who sounds as though he or she is talking directly to the listener. It is also the only advertising medium that can paint vivid, memorable word pictures in listeners' minds.

Since most people listen in their cars, radio can have immediate impact on the actions of consumers. There are lots of stories about people driving down the street, hearing an ad for a store, and going directly to the store to buy. I've done it, and I'll bet you have, too.

With radio, frequency is absolutely essential. A retailer who only wants to run an occasional spot shouldn't bother. The more often your prospective customers hear your spot, the more likely they are to respond. A retailer friend of mine ran four or five spots on a local morning drive radio show for several years. He stopped for a couple of weeks to rethink his campaign and to create some new spots. Since they hadn't heard his radio spots for a couple of days, several regular customers called to ask if he was going out of business.

TELEVISION

Television is the granddaddy of retail advertising media. A well-conceived TV campaign can have tremendous impact. When considering TV advertising, it's important to understand the differences between broadcast and cable. Broadcast TV has dominated America's living rooms for more than 50 years. Today, with so many of the nation's households wired for cable, the emphasis is shifting to the broad variety of cable channels. This is very good news for retailers because you can now target your message to consumers who are most likely to buy.

What is so amazing about cable TV advertising is, retailers no longer have to spend vast amounts of money on production costs to be successful. Gallery Furniture in Houston has become one of the most successful furniture stores in the country with Jim McIngvale's low-budget TV commercials. Countless other retailers have done the same.

This does not mean down-and-dirty, low-budget cable TV spots will work for every kind of store. Logic says this approach won't work if you are trying to sell high-ticket merchandise to an upscale customer. Unfortunately, a good many of the cable TV commercials developed by upscale retailers cost far more than they should, and spending a lot on production costs does not guarantee success. You can be successful using cable TV by creating a powerful message, targeting the audience you want to reach, and delivering the message as frequently as your budget will allow.

Most cable TV homes receive 60 or more channels, so targeting becomes easier all the time. If you want to reach the people who watch professional wrestling, you can do it with cable TV. If you want to reach the people who watch reruns of "The Brady Bunch," you can do it with cable TV.

The opportunities are endless. If your targeted customers are PBS viewers, look for opportunities to sponsor specific programs.

OUTDOOR

For many years I was against the use of billboards as an advertising medium for retailers—that is until I saw how the folks at The Container Store used them to build their business. They proved to me that with a creative approach and the right billboard locations, a retailer can benefit greatly. If you have multiple stores and lifestyle-oriented merchandise, I encourage you to consider using billboards.

INTERNET

I would be foolish to write about the various ways for retailers to advertise and not address the Internet. Internet banner advertising can be an important medium for advertisers. One thing that makes banner ads so appealing is their ability not only to target a specific customer or group of customers, but to get direct feedback or even a sale. It is simply the most interactive form of advertising ever devised. Best of all, you can measure and evaluate how many and, in some situations, who sees your ad. You may not want to put a great deal of advertising dollars into Internet banners, but it's certainly worth testing whether it will work for your stores.

COMBINING MEDIA

One thing the most savvy retail advertisers have learned in recent years is how to combine daily newspaper advertising with a series of TV spots, or TV spots with radio spots, or newspaper with radio. Cross-supporting ads can produce spectacular results and often produce sales far above what the two mediums produce when used separately.

For combination campaign success, be sure the messages are congruent. They must fit together and support a common theme. We've seen it time and time again—sales go up when the customer first hears the advertising message on the radio and then reads it in the newspaper. Sales go up when the customer sees the advertising message on TV and also hears it on radio. Sales go up when the customer hears the advertising message on the radio and then receives a direct-mail piece. As is the case with all advertising, planning and timing are important.

◆

CHAPTER 20

ATTACK THE HOLIDAY SELLING OPPORTUNITIES

ustomers who have never been in your store before will walk through your doors during the holiday season. These new customers present an opportunity for you not only to build sales during the holidays but also to build a relationship that generates sales well into the future. Will they know how to find what they're looking for? Will they know what merchandise and services you offer in your store? Will they know what merchandise is on sale, or

◆

what's being featured? Or will they leave without buying anything at all?

OPPORTUNITY #1
Make it easy for customers to shop in your stores!

If you are not already doing so, the holiday season is a great time of year to put a greeter at the front door to welcome customers and give them a map of the store or a list of specials or featured items. If a greeter is inappropriate for your store, you may wish to put up posters of the store's layout or have a stack of maps near the entrance. In surveys and among consumer research panelists, one of the most common reasons customers give for not buying is their inability to find specific merchandise or departments in stores. How easy is it for customers to find what they're looking for in your store?

OPPORTUNITY #2
Offer your customers a one-of-a-kind shopping experience!

It's a great time during the final weeks of the year to provide unique services for your holiday shoppers. Throughout the year, stores serving upper income consumers offer such services as merchandise delivery, special gift wrapping, valet parking, and even personal shoppers to help customers make the best choices. Other retailers have found that offering these kinds of services during the holidays not only provides a one-of-a-kind holiday shopping experience for their customers but also gives them a real competitive edge.

OPPORTUNITY #3
Teach employees the importance of good service to holiday shoppers!

The level of customer service even in the best stores often slips during the holiday season. Sales associates, cashiers, and managers can be overwhelmed by the number of customers they must help all at the same time. With so much activity in the store, some customers fail to get the level of service they expect. The results are unhappy shoppers and lost sales.

A good number of multi-store retailers kick off the holiday season with managers' meetings, regional training programs for store personnel, holiday sales rallies, or special holiday kick-off events in each store. The purpose of these pre-holiday meetings can vary. It may simply be to get everyone excited about the upcoming season or to talk about the company's merchandising and marketing strategies for the season. Or the purpose may be to remind everyone of the importance of serving customers and getting them focused on ways to maximize sales during those all-important final weeks of the year. Take some time to help sales associates understand the importance of good service. Even short, small group or one-on-one training sessions can pay real dividends.

OPPORTUNITY #4
Hold daily store meetings with sales associates!

I've found that managers who have meetings with their associates at least once a week avoid misunderstandings about what is expected of them. As a bonus, these managers generally have better relationships with their salespeople. To take advantage of the opportunities available during the last few weeks of the year, I encourage you to take this idea one step further and hold store meetings every day. They may only last a few minutes, but can have a profound impact on your people and how they serve your holiday customers.

One store manager I know holds 15- to 20-minute daily store meetings starting the middle of November. She talks about the previous day's sales numbers and congratulates everyone who reached their goal. If they didn't make their numbers, she asks them to make a commitment to pay attention to every customer, give every shopper an opportunity to buy add-on and accessory merchandise, and work a little harder so the store will reach that day's goal.

She celebrates the accomplishments of associates with the highest sales numbers for the previous day. She talks about merchandise that may be in short supply, items that need a little push, new merchandise that arrived the previous day, and merchandise that is featured in the company's advertising that week. She ends every daily meeting with an inspirational quote, poem, or a thought that will help her salespeople work just a little harder, sell more merchandise, and serve customers better that day.

OPPORTUNITY #5
Hold daily meetings with store managers!

Beginning the day after Thanksgiving, the owner of an eight-store chain in California has a short meeting with his store managers at the end of each day to talk about what happened that day and how they can do better the next day. Since his stores are not far from each other, meetings are usually held at the company's flagship location. On days when schedules won't permit a face-to-face meeting, the owner and managers have a conference call at the end of the day.

These daily sessions keep everyone focused on sales goals, hot-selling merchandise, and how best to maximize and shift inventory between stores. Even though they are always tired at the end of the day, the managers find the daily meeting to be a great way to share what is working, what they need to do better, and what they are doing individually to achieve their goals. Each manager has a sales goal for his or her own store, and because the owner runs contests for the highest percentage sales increases, there's some good-natured bragging and bantering between managers throughout the season. The daily meetings present a terrific opportunity for everyone to focus on increasing sales.

OPPORTUNITY #6
Use contests to put excitement
in the selling process!

Daily and weekly sales contests are a way of life in some retail segments. Consumer electronics, furniture, and menswear retailers frequently have sales contests on their busiest days of the week and offer everything from cash prizes or merchandise discounts to concert tickets or dinner at a local restaurant. If you aren't using sales contests on a regular basis in your stores, try using them during the holiday season. It's a terrific opportunity to put some real excitement into the selling process.

Keep this in mind. Individual prizes don't have to be expensive. They do have to be motivational and reward real achievement. You can offer a prize for the first big sale over a certain dollar amount. You can reward the associate with the most sales for the day, the sale with the most items, and just about anything else that will get everyone involved and excited about selling.

A men's and women's apparel store manager tapes sealed envelopes on the inside of his office door at the beginning of each day during the holiday season. The envelopes contain $1, $5, $10, or $20 bills. Whenever associates make a sale over $100, they write their names on one of the envelopes, not knowing how much it contains. The more sales they make, the more often their names appear on envelopes

At the end of the day, the associates get all the envelopes with their names on them and eagerly open them to see how much cash they earned in the contest that day. This type of daily sales contest is popular with associates not only because of the extra cash they can earn but also because it creates a great deal of excitement in the store and focuses everyone on selling.

OPPORTUNITY #7
Remerchandise and create new displays often to stimulate sales!

Attacking opportunities during the holidays also means making sure your store is well-merchandised throughout the season. Over the last few years a growing number of savvy retailers have been remerchandising their stores several times throughout the season. Some create new displays with different products as often as every week. Others bring in completely new merchandise featuring different price points as the season progresses. If it is appropriate in your stores, you may find that remerchandising several times throughout the season will help stimulate sales.

During the last few days before Christmas, you may find it helpful to prewrap some of your merchandise. This is a great way to boost sales of even poor-selling items. Last year a client of mine had a very slow-mover early in the season and took it off the floor for a couple of weeks. He then had nearly all of these items prewrapped and created a large display for them located in a prominent position the weekend before Christmas. He sold the entire inventory in two days.

BRAINSTORMING YOUR ATTACK!

As you get closer to the holiday season, spend time looking around your stores. Talk with managers, assistants, and sales associates about how best to maximize this year's holiday opportunities. Look for ways everyone can contribute to your store's success, and attack the opportunities.

CHAPTER 21

STRATEGIES, ATTITUDES, AND ACTIONS THAT LIMIT SUCCESS!

What are the reasons for retail success? Is it good planning or that a company has been in business for many years? No doubt there are benefits to being in business for a long time. Online retailers that were well-financed in the early stages of their existence hoped that would ensure their success. But some exceptionally well-funded startups have failed miserably.

Retail success does not occur just because of hundreds

of millions of dollars in IPO and venture-capital money alone. It's far more complicated.

Retail success is about the strategies that are adopted and executed, the actions taken, and the attitudes of people managing and working in the business. It is also about understanding these strategies, actions, and attitudes—and how they can lead to great success or as sometimes happens, how they can limit success.

SUCCESS LIMITER #1
A lack of clear focus!

There has been a great deal written about how important corporate and leadership vision is to business success. But vision alone is not enough. RadioShack ran a full-page ad in *The Wall Street Journal* when it announced the company's name change from Tandy Corp. The headline read, "There is no vision without focus."

A lack of clear focus is very evident in a company's strategy, daily actions, and in the attitudes of its people. As a strategy, the most successful retailers are obsessive about clearly focusing their entire business in a direction or on a segment of the industry. That obsession includes everything from the selection of merchandise and marketing communications to store design and the customers' in-store experiences. Even successful mass merchants must clearly focus on serving the needs of a specific group of consumers.

Wal-Mart's focus is on America's largest population group—middle and lower income, value-driven consumers. The execution of that focus is very clear in Wal-Mart stores and in their advertising. Target's focus is on serving a more upscale—middle to upper income—value-driven group of consumers. Everything from store locations and merchandise selection to the company's involvement with a number of charities supports the focus.

Since most of my work is with specialty retailers, I often witness the struggle some specialty operations experience because of a lack of focus. It may be they aren't focusing on a specific group of consumers. Or they may not have a clear merchandising focus, value proposition, and overall business purpose. One of the first questions I ask is, "What is the purpose of your business?" The answers I get include "to generate more profit, grow the business, and increase stockholder value." While these are perfectly good goals, they are not the real purpose of a business.

When asked this question, a jewelry retailer answered, "To provide customers with merchandise they can't find elsewhere, at fair prices, and make sure they have a good time shopping in our stores." Good answer!

Both The Sports Authority and John Morris's Bass Pro Shop stores are big-box sporting goods retailers, but a visit to their stores and conversations with their staff will demonstrate the differences between them quite clearly. Sports Authority offers a massive selection in a mostly self-service environment. The company's advertising, store layouts, and merchandising approach differ little from other mass merchants. The overall focus is sporting goods; the purpose is unclear.

Bass Pro Shops also offer a massive selection of merchandise. The difference is the shopping environment. The stores are spectacular, with ponds and waterfalls; there are wonderful merchandise displays, and the sales associates are friendly and knowledgeable. The purpose of these stores is quite clear.

Focus is also an attitude. One of the personal characteristics often found among entrepreneurs is that they get bored once the major start-up challenges of the business have been overcome and the company is successful. Then, the founder often looks for new challenges.

This change in focus can spread to the others—the individuals who are responsible for continuing to build the business. If the owner or senior executive is not clearly focused on the continuing growth and success of the company, that lack of or change in focus can impact how everyone else approaches the business.

SUCCESS LIMITER #2
Our customers are different!

Everyone thinks their customers are different. There was a time when higher-income customers would have done anything to avoid shopping in discount stores. No longer. There was a time when lower-income customers would have stayed away from Beverly Hills and other shopping destinations with high-priced boutiques. No longer.

Consumers make decisions about stores and the merchandise they buy based on their own uniquely personal priorities and values. A customer who buys an $80,000 luxury car might be the same customer who pumps his own gas to save a nickel a gallon. A customer who buys a designer dress at an exclusive boutique might buy matching shoes at a self-service, discount store.

To make judgments about where customers will shop and what they will buy based on their age, income, address, or other purely demographic factors is very dangerous indeed. Successful retailers understand that anyone with even the slightest interest in their merchandise is a potential customer.

Our business is different!

A variation on this limitation is, "Our business is different!" Whether you sell your merchandise in a small or a large store, or in a competitive or not-so-competitive marketplace, the everyday challenges you face are remarkably similar to those of every other retailer. You must constantly find ways to:

- Attract more customers.

- Sell more merchandise.

- Sell it more profitably.

- Keep the merchandise fresh and exciting.

- Manage the inventory investment efficiently.

- Manage hundreds of other details.

- Improve every aspect of the business.

What separates the most successful retail companies from the mediocre ones is that they learn from their mistakes and adopt business-building ideas and practices from other companies, regardless of the industry. While you may not be in the same business as Apple Computer, there is a great deal to be learned from the company's extraordinary turnaround. Apple went from near bankruptcy to exceptional quarterly and yearly growth. With regard to Apple's newest products, the corporation has done what other computer hardware companies have never done before. Apple has created products that don't look like everyone else's, and the company injected humor and fun into a segment not known for humor or fun.

Our industry is different!

Another variation on this limitation is, "Our industry is different!" Yes, selling hardware is different from selling women's apparel. But does the customer who visits the hardware store looking for a shelf bracket for her pantry on one day have different expectations the next day when she goes into a jewelry store to have her watch battery replaced? She expects to find an attractive, well-designed store; attentive, knowledgeable sales associates; good service; and fair prices.

The "our industry is different" mind-set leads to all kinds of business limitations. It keeps retailers from making the kinds of changes that are necessary to distinguish their stores from the competition. It keeps retailers from pushing the boundaries and trying new things. And it keeps retailers from taking their business to a higher level of performance.

Imagine you were an unseen observer when Les Wexner first proposed buying a small two-store San Francisco retail company and creating a national chain of boutiques selling sexy lingerie to women all across America. In those days lingerie was only sold in department stores and small neighborhood boutiques—not in beautifully designed Victoria's Secret mall stores.

Imagine you were an unseen observer when the people at Victoria's Secret proposed they hold their annual fashion shows live on the Internet—the second of which was broadcast from the Cannes Film Festival in France. These shows have attracted hundreds of thousands of Web visitors.

Sure, your industry is different, but if you act and function just like every other retailer in your industry, you're going to limit your success.

SUCCESS LIMITER #3
Low expectations!

In a marketplace where competitors are looking for ways to capture more business every day, retailers who aren't constantly improving are doomed. Every day, as we go through life, we see mediocre work, poor performance, sloppy execution, and too many people who fail to deliver the kind of service customers expect. As I stand before audiences around the country and talk about customer service, I hear horror stories about all kinds of companies. When I first started back in the 1980s, those stories most often were about little-known companies. Today, the stories I hear are about some of the country's most revered companies. Retailers on every level need to raise their performance expectations for everything from corporate efficiency to customer service to sales.

ONGOING TRAINING AND DEVELOPMENT

Improving performance is more than just generating more sales. I had a conversation with a seasoned, well-accomplished sales associate not long ago who told me his manager regularly visited the various departments in the store telling associates when they had failed to hit their goal for the previous day. Instead of focusing on what the associates could do to reach the goal today, she wanted to know why they hadn't done it yesterday. Her entire focus was on the store's daily sales numbers rather than on the performance of each person and how she might help that person improve.

As an executive, owner, or manager, raise your own expectations and then help your people raise their performance to meet those expectations. In the last few years, more and more retail companies have realized the value of investing in the training and education of their managers and associates. The next step: raise the performance you expect from the better trained managers and associates. Those retail companies that haven't yet committed to providing their people with ongoing training and development will find it very difficult to significantly raise performance levels. It's easy enough to say you expect more, but until you make the effort to train and develop your people, you won't get more.

EXPECTING LESS, ACCEPTING LESS

One of the most basic operational strategies of chain-store retailing is to open as many stores as possible as quickly as possible. This allows the organization to take advantage of mass buying opportunities, spreading the cost of everything from advertising to administration among as many stores as possible.

But another thing occurs when retailers open all those stores. While it certainly isn't intentional, the performance expectations often end up being lower for the additional stores than they were for the first one or two. The reasoning is that the new stores can't possibly perform at the same level as the flagship store, and they aren't expected to. Why not?

The acceptance that any store cannot achieve maximum performance costs retailers millions of dollars in lost revenues and profits every single day. When a retail organization raises performance expectations and supports the higher level by training employees, making sure stores are fully stocked, and offering an exceptional shopping experience for every customer, nothing can stop their success.

SUCCESS LIMITER #4
I like to keep a close eye on things!

For many years one of the nation's most successful independent retailers ran his business with this philosophy. He could only keep an eye on what was happening in one store so, rather than expand a winning concept, he chose to avoid adding more locations. That one store was extremely successful, but his desire to maintain absolute control over the business was holding him back. He finally realized this and is now getting ready to open additional stores.

By any measure, management control is a double-edged sword. To achieve great success, management must take control over the business, set standards, guide the direction, and make the decisions that impact the company's growth. At the same time, the most successful retailers spend a great deal of time and effort finding and hiring talented people, teaching them how to do their jobs, and executing the company's plans.

MENTORING

I am a very strong advocate of mentoring. Building a successful retail business depends on how effectively owners and senior executives guide, teach, and counsel the people around them. An effective mentor shows his or her employees how to think and act in a way that reflects the company's values and beliefs. Mentoring doesn't just take place during weekly meetings or phone conversations. It requires hours and hours of talking, sharing insights, showing how the business should be managed, and helping the mentee think and act like a retailer.

If you hire the best, most talented people you can find and give them the education, support, and tools they need to do the job, the next step is to get out of the way and let them help you build a successful business.

SUCCESS LIMITER #5
Poor communication!

In my conversations with people at every level—from front-line associates to senior executives—the one success limiter I hear about most often is poor communication between individuals, departments, and stores.

The most successful store managers spend countless hours each week keeping their salespeople informed about what is expected of them, what's going on in the company, problems that may need to be resolved, how best to deal with out-of-stock situations, and, quite literally, hundreds of other issues.

A company's communication problems usually begin with the owner or highest level executive. If that person decides the salespeople don't need to know, they won't. I see managers who spend too much time in their offices talking with other managers on the phone, failing to keep their associates abreast of what's going on.

One of the characteristics that sets The Container Store apart from so many other retail companies is the communication among all levels of the organization. Every day store associates get sales results from the previous day. Every day they're told what their own sales goals are as well as for the store overall. Founders Kip Tindall and Garret Boone share a great deal of information with their associates. The result not only is the continued growth they've enjoyed year after year, but recognition by *Fortune* magazine as the "Best company to work for in America" for two consecutive years.

Poor communication also causes problems when senior-level managers and executives assume that the people working in stores know what the company stands for, believes in, and why they are in business. You may have a couple of days devoted to initial orientation and training—and maybe even a nice little booklet that tells about the history of the company. But these things do not go far enough. Creating a retail organization of employees who know and understand the company's business, purpose, values, and principles requires ongoing communication. It requires constant dialogue and a process for making sure everyone understands the goals, the achievements, and the focus on building the business.

RECOGNIZE AND UNDERSTAND THE LIMITATIONS!

Every business has strategies, actions, and attitudes that can get in the way of success. The key is to recognize their existence and take steps to eliminate them. It's tough enough to build a business in today's fiercely competitive climate without doing things that limit your company's success.

CHAPTER
22

SETTING THE STAGE FOR THE NEW RETAIL ECONOMY!

I n just a few short years, the Internet has become the most important new communication, sales, marketing, and business-building tool of our time. With hundreds of thousands of Web sites and millions of pages available online, it is no longer enough just to have a Web site. To succeed in the economy of the 21st century, retailers must embrace eCommerce and use the technology as an integral part of their total business strategy.

Retailers already know that to do business in this economy, they must constantly improve every aspect of how they serve customers. And they know that fundamentally sound management is essential to surviving in a highly competitive environment. What some retailers have had difficulty accepting is that constant change is, and will continue to be, an integral part of doing business. This is particularly true when the change is driven by a completely new concept like the Internet. Witness these last few years to see how the Internet is fast proving its importance not only as a technological advancement but also as an essential tool for building a retail business.

A HIGH-STAKES RACE!

The business of selling to and serving consumers went through a massive change in the mid-1900s when retailers abandoned downtown streets for suburban shopping centers. While thousands of retailers enjoyed tremendous growth by moving into malls, others that failed to make the move just muddled along for a few years or disappeared from the retail landscape.

Later in the century, retailing changed again when Wal-Mart and Kmart began opening giant discount stores all across America. Retailers who failed to understand what was occurring—and didn't reposition their stores for a different retail environment—disappeared. Then, in the 1980s, such big-box specialty stores as Home Depot, Office

Depot, Best Buy, and PetsMart began spreading across the country. And again, the retailers who failed did so either because they didn't recognize this fundamental change in the marketplace or didn't have the ability, wherewithal, or desire to do anything about it.

In every era, there have been fundamental changes leading to great success for some and failure for others. This new retail economy is no exception.

INTERNET IMPACT!

Here we are again going through a period of great change; one in which some companies will enjoy tremendous success and others will fail. Internet companies already have considerable impact on widely diverse merchandise categories and services.

One example of the Internet's impact is in the antiques business. According to antiques retailers from coast to coast, the success of online auction site eBay is directly attributable to measurable declines in their own store traffic and profits. With millions of visitors every month, eBay has become the world's largest outlet for antiques and collectibles. If these antiques retailers don't embrace the Internet or redefine how they do business, there surely will be failures among their ranks.

Over the next five years, most retail segments will experience this same impact in varying degrees. In the comfort of their homes and offices, consumers can buy such easy-to-compare items as music videos and CDs, books, cosmetics, shoes, toys, flowers, sporting goods, golf clubs, and clothes. And now, a growing number of consumers research and buy hard-to-find items including antiques, collectibles, clothing in hard-to-find sizes, art, unique food items, tools, and just about any kind of merchandise one can imagine. They also are doing the research and arranging online home mortgages, car loans, and vacations. They're buying stocks and using a wide range of personal services.

Unlike other times in business history, this battle is not solely between small and large companies. It is much more about forward-thinking business people who are willing to take bold steps. It is about thinking differently by communicating with, selling to, and serving customers. It is about challenging everything you do every day and being unafraid to embrace new ideas, strategies, and methods.

INTERNET MYTHS!

One of the widely held myths of the last several years is that if you don't already have an Internet presence and your Web site isn't up and running now, you are too late. It turns out, this statement—made by various companies already online and some so-called Internet experts—is simply nonsense. There are still opportunities for retailers to establish a presence on the Internet, create sites that attract Web visitors, and sell substantial quantities of merchandise.

Another Internet myth is that online sales will never

account for more than 5 percent or 10 percent of overall retail sales. In the $3 trillion retail industry, 5 percent or 10 percent of the marketplace is hardly insignificant. I wouldn't want to bet that it will be limited to that percentage either.

In some categories of merchandise, the numbers are already exploding, and they could very well represent more than 25 percent of the marketplace in the next few years. Retailers who discount the importance of the Internet and believe it won't hurt their businesses are in for a rude awakening.

THE BRICK-AND-MORTAR FUTURE!

Everyone in business has heard the predictions that retail stores had better look out: Online merchants will put them all out of business. That's absurd! Consumers still love to shop in stores; they enjoy the experience. They enjoy being around other people. And they enjoy touching the merchandise. A well-known brick-and-mortar retailer with an established customer base has a tremendous advantage over a pure-play Internet startup or any other startup.

Just as in the past, brick-and-mortar retailers who fail to offer the customer something truly special in the way of convenience, merchandise, service, pricing, or shopping experience will disappear. Brick-and-mortar retailers who understand this and offer customers compelling reasons to do business with them, whether online or off, will thrive in the new retail economy.

WHAT IS THE NEW RETAIL ECONOMY?

The new retail economy uses new technologies with old sales and marketing concepts to sell to and serve consumers.

Recorded history describes auctions as far back as 500 BC. But at no time in history has there ever been anything quite like online auctions. Attracting staggering numbers of visitors every day, eBay (www.eBay.com) is one of the busiest sites on the Web, selling billions of dollars worth of merchandise each year.

Online auctions are just one old concept that's being revived on the Internet. For years retailers selling everything from furniture and automobiles to jewelry and consumer electronics have tried to distance themselves from the old haggling way to sell. A lot of consumer electronics retailers have only been able to move from negotiated to fixed pricing in the last five or 10 years.

Now, we have such Internet companies as Priceline.com that use bidding and a negotiated pricing model to attract buyers of airline tickets, home mortgages, automobiles, and more. The Internet will continue to redefine traditional retail pricing models and has already shown it will serve as a medium for entirely new ways to price and sell goods and services.

In the new retail economy, narrowly niched retailers operate innovative Web sites that sell unique merchandise.

The Internet may be one of the great equalizers of all time. It is simply the best opportunity I've seen for specialty retailers to grow quickly—selling to consumers all around the world. A great site operated by a narrowly niched specialty retailer is Guitars and Cadillacs, based in Texas (www.BuyTexasOnline.com). No, this site doesn't sell guitars or Cadillacs, but it does sell just about anything you can imagine from the State of Texas. Both the stores and Web site offer such items as Texas food, gift baskets, apparel, and home furnishings. If you've always wanted a framed flag of Texas to hang on your wall or a stained glass star of Texas, this is the place to get it.

Gadzooks (www.gadzooks.com), another narrowly niched retailer, operates one of the more creatively designed sites on the Web. Gadzooks, with more than 300 stores in malls all across the United States, sells casual apparel for young (13- to 19-year-old) men and women. The site features information on the company and a store locator. It has the kind of creative look and feel young consumers find appealing.

In the new retail economy, retailers and manufacturers create newly defined and mutually beneficial relationships that serve consumers better.

Levi Strauss announced at the end of 1999 that it would stop selling Levi products on its own Web site, a reversal of the company's earlier restrictions that limited online sales to the Levi Strauss site alone. *Forbes* categorized Levi's decision as the first major brand to surrender in the cyber wars. *Forbes* was wrong.

Levi's decision to reverse this policy more likely was based on the realization that it was a mistake trying to be the exclusive online retailer of Levi products. The original restrictions eliminated the opportunity to partner with retailers and would have cost the company far more in the long term than it would have gained by selling direct to consumers online. This time Levi Strauss made the right decision not only for itself but also for consumers and retailers as well.

Among the more common uses of retailer/manufacturer partnerships on the Web is dealer or retailer locator services on manufacturer Web sites. Taylor Made Golf Company's Web site (www.taylormadegolf.com) provides links that consumers can use to access on-course pro shops, golf retailers, and pure-play eCommerce sites. Black & Decker's Web site (www.blackanddecker.com) includes descriptions of the company's larger retail partners, displays their logos, and provides links to their Web sites. Among Black &

Decker's retail partners are Lowe's, Home Depot, Payless Cashways, Ace Hardware, and True Value.

Manufacturers are beginning to take steps to use the Internet to create real partnerships with their retailers. The opportunities can include closed-access Web sites that allow retailers to check availability, track order and shipping status, access product information, obtain in-store plan-o-gram suggestions, and handle a whole range of communication issues. The manufacturer can also share data on consumer buying patterns, pricing strategies, and anything else that will help the retailer partners increase merchandise sales.

In the new retail economy, manufacturers of products—from computers to apparel—sell directly to consumers on the Web, in their own stores, and through other retailers.

Computers and other technological products are probably the best examples of how manufacturers create vertical operations. Such companies as Dell, Gateway, Hewlett-Packard, Adobe, and Compaq sell merchandise directly to the end user via catalogs, Web sites, inbound telephone operations and, for some, their own stores. The Gap, The Limited, Eddie Bauer, Abercrombie & Fitch, and other apparel retailers have long sourced their merchandise and sold it in their own stores and catalogs. These retailers have now added Web sites to the mix.

There is a wide range of retailers and manufacturers

expanding on this multi-channel approach to selling and serving customers. The driving force is the ability to more effectively serve specific, highly targeted consumer groups and lifestyles.

It's hard to argue with the fact that there are too many stores, too many catalogs, and now, too many Web sites. In such an overcrowded marketplace, a highly focused selection of merchandise, a unique pricing approach, and a convenient way to shop that are all geared toward a specific group of customers may be the best strategy for building a successful retail business in the future.

IT'S AN EXCEPTIONAL TIME TO BE A RETAILER!

We are doing business in one of history's most exciting times. The opportunities to grow our businesses, sell more merchandise, serve more customers, and have a heck of a lot of fun doing it have never been better. Those who stick their heads in the sand and fail to embrace this new retail economy are going to miss out.

CHAPTER
23

◆

A MATTER OF RELEVANCE

The business of selling to and serving consumers is changing faster today that it has in the last 50 years. But the importance of relevance in retail is something that will never change whether you operate brick-and-mortar stores, catalogs, or an eCommerce Web site. If your business is relevant to people and how they live their lives, you dramatically increase your chances for success. If your business is extremely relevant, you will be extremely successful.

◆

CHICKEN-SOUP RELEVANCE

Let me give you an example of a relevant business. Several years ago, a couple of moderately successful professional speakers—Mark Victor Hansen and Jack Canfield—came upon an idea for a book. The book was to include stories from real people about events that had touched, influenced, or even changed their lives. Today, the *Chicken Soup for the Soul* books have sold millions of copies, and, needless to say, Mark and Jack are wildly successful. There's no denying these two guys are very good marketers. But what has made the *Chicken Soup for the Soul* concept so successful is the simple fact that the stories being told are relevant to hundreds of thousands of people all over the world.

LUMBERYARD RELEVANCE

Relevance can be seen both in very large companies and very small. Several years ago, the owner of a single-location lumber and building materials business looked around and saw that if he didn't take some steps soon, it wouldn't be long before he would be up against some very large competitors. Midwest powerhouse Menard's was moving in his direction and Home Depot wasn't far behind.

So, the first thing he did was begin opening his lumberyard at 5:00 a.m. This allowed contractors and other workers to stop by and pick up the things they needed for their jobs early in the day. He also put in a big coffee pot and offered free doughnuts and pastries so his customers wouldn't have to make another stop between their homes and his lumberyard.

Contractors and workers from all around the area soon discovered he was open early and had free coffee and doughnuts. Within a few months, the parking lot was packed every morning. It wasn't long before these tradesmen began talking with each other and the yard's owner about their projects and the challenges they faced in running their businesses.

Among their biggest challenges were such things as getting financing for projects, trying to manage the financial aspects of their businesses more effectively, along with other business management issues. Being a resourceful fellow, the lumberyard owner began offering seminars to his customers on these subjects. He also arranged to have bankers show up at the yard early in the morning to get to know the customers and talk with them about their financing needs.

The results of these efforts have been profound. Today Menard's and Home Depot both do business in his community. But since the owner and his single store have become so important to the contractors in that community, the business continues to flourish. He has touched their lives by doing more than just sell them merchandise. He has become extremely relevant.

WHEN IS A COMPANY
NO LONGER RELEVANT?

When Montgomery Ward emerged from bankruptcy in 1999, reporters from several daily newspapers around the country called asking me to comment on the company's chances for success. The newly remodeled stores had a more open format, better signage and graphics, and generally a more attractive look. While operating in bankruptcy, the company refocused its merchandise selection on apparel and moved away from consumer electronics, all of which made Wards a better store than before. But the big question was whether Wards could be successful serving the same customers as JCPenney, Kohl's, Sears, Target, Kmart, and many other retailers. This is a question all retailers should ask themselves:

- Can we be successful serving the same customers lots of other retailers serve?

I believe the issue with Wards was whether they were taking steps to become relevant to consumers. Here are some other questions that should be asked:

- Are we an important part of our customers' lives?

- Are our stores places where they want to go to shop and spend time?

- Do our customers feel comfortable, welcome, and wanted in our stores?

- Do they really like or even love our merchandise?

- Are our customers proud to own the merchandise they buy from us?

- Does the merchandise meet and exceed their expectations?

- Do they like the people who work in our stores?

- Are they getting real value when they shop in our stores?

- Do they think the prices are fair and reasonable?

- Is our store a relevant part of our customers' lives or could they shop in another store and get the same merchandise at the same prices?

It turns out that Wards was unable to reestablish itself as a viable retail business forcing management to close the stores and liquidate the 128-year-old company. Customers no longer cared about doing business with Wards. They were no longer relevant.

IF YOUR STORE DISAPPEARED TOMORROW, WOULD IT MAKE ANY DIFFERENCE AT ALL TO YOUR CUSTOMERS?

With too many stores, too many catalogs, and too many Web sites, how relevant your store and your merchandise is in your customers' lives may be the most important challenge you face right now. I'm sure you've read all kinds of stories about Nordstrom's famous customer service. I believe a more important factor in Nordstrom's success is how they've become so much a part of their customers' lives. Nordstrom customers absolutely love shopping in Nordstrom stores. They love the merchandise. They love the people.

Hallmark Gold Crown store owners tell me they have customers who visit their stores every week to see what's new and even spend a little time just hanging around. These customers love the store and its merchandise.

I've been critical of amazon.com's inability to generate a profit, but they deserve credit for creating a Web site that people love to visit. There may be no better place in the world to find books on any subject. That makes them relevant. On the other end of the spectrum are the great Barnes & Noble brick-and-mortar stores. Although they both sell books, Barnes & Noble's relevance is different than amazon.com's. Customers love shopping in the kind of atmosphere found in the Barnes & Noble stores.

Not long ago McDonald's opened its 25,000th restaurant. People were asked why they ate there, and every single person interviewed said how much they loved McDonald's. Now, I don't know of anyone who thinks McDonald's has the world's best food, but millions of people eat there every day because it is a relevant part of their lives.

RELEVANCE IS MORE THAN A GREAT LOOKING STORE!

In other chapters in this book, I've written about how

such companies as REI, Bass Pro Shops, Disney Stores, and the like have been able to distinguish themselves by creating dynamic looking stores. I have also written about how retailers like Gallery Furniture have distinguished themselves with unique ways to sell merchandise at great prices.

Creating a unique business model that leads to success nearly always fosters a whole batch of copy-cat companies. Soon after Sol Price's first Price Clubs began to enjoy success, a number of imitators sprung up around the country. The same was true when Victoria's Secret first began opening their lingerie boutiques. Copy cats will always be around. And with few truly unique retail concepts or business models, what can a retailer do to become and remain relevant to consumers?

MARKETING

In an effort to become more relevant to their customers, many retailers create highly segmented databases that allow them to offer specific merchandise to customers who are most interested in the merchandise. This is certainly one of the things such conventional retailers as Neiman Marcus and eCommerce retailers like amazon.com do best. As we move forward, the one-to-one marketing concepts pioneered by Martha Rogers and Don Peppers (authors of *The One to One Future* and *Enterprise One to One*) will be an integral part of how specialty retailers do business.

COMMUNITY INVOLVEMENT

I have long advocated that retailers get involved in their communities by sponsoring and contributing to charitable events or educational programs. Charitable events and educational programs touch everyone's lives, and retailers who take part in them become more relevant to the people in the community.

STORE EMPLOYEES

How customers think of your sales associates has an enormous impact on your relevance. When they have made a connection with the people working in your store, they'll shop more often and buy more. When they are greeted by name and made to feel wanted and welcome, they'll shop more often and buy more.

When someone smiles at them, makes eye contact, and says "hello," they'll shop more often and buy more. When the store is more than a place selling merchandise and becomes a place where serving customers is the driving force in the operation of the business, they'll shop more often and buy more.

MANAGEMENT

As I look at retail companies all across the country, I see many that lack relevance. They may have lots of great merchandise beautifully displayed, but is that enough? My wife and I went into a Container Store and a happy, funny woman greeted us. She not only made us feel welcome but also made us laugh and have a good time shopping there. I know that owners Kip Tindell and Garrett Boone are the reason that employee was so good at what she did, because they genuinely care about being relevant to their customers.

On a trip to Houston, Texas, a couple of years ago, I bought some clothes from Harold's in the Heights, an exceptional family owned menswear store. I was served by Harold Wiesenthal's son, Michael, who genuinely cares about being relevant to his customers. Another customer shopping that day had driven to the store from West Texas, more than 100 miles away, to buy a suit at Harold's. I'm sure there are plenty of places between West Texas and Houston to buy suits, but he came to Harold's because that store and the people working there are relevant to him.

For your stores to be relevant, you must do more than just sell merchandise; you must touch people's lives!

THE BEST OF
THE BEST

As you've probably noticed by now, throughout this book I repeatedly emphasize the importance of distinguishing your store from every other store in the marketplace. Sometimes the unique way a retailer defines the business from its inception can be the determining factor. For some of the nation's most distinguishable stores, the basic business concept was clearly defined from the earliest days.

For example, in 1987 when Howard Schultz bought the Starbucks Coffee Company in Seattle, his vision was clear. He wanted to open coffee shops and retail stores all across the country that would be more than just a store. It also would be a meeting place for people to have coffee and spend time with friends. This idea was based on the coffee shops he'd seen on a trip to Italy several years before. Today, Starbucks is one of the world's most successful retail concepts. It provides people with a unique environment and a comfortable place to have coffee and socialize.

Starbucks built a successful business from a well-defined concept. That is not the case with many other retail companies. It is more common for a concept to evolve over several years, maybe starting with the desire to sell a specific category of merchandise or to offer general merchandise in a big-box store or at reduced prices. In a marketplace with hundreds of thousands of stores, virtually every kind of specialty category, and more so-called discounters than anyone could ever have imagined, what can a retail business that's already well-established do to stand out from the crowd?

You do not merely want to be considered just the best of the best. You want to be considered the only ones who do what you do. —JERRY GARCIA

How can already successful retailers move their businesses from ordinary to extraordinary; from the point of being like every other business in the community to where they are "...considered the only ones who do what they do."

Over the last few years, Hallmark Cards has worked with their Gold Crown retailers to become the only ones who do what they do in the card and gift business. Together they have built a network of card and gift stores that defines the category much like Starbucks does in the coffee business.

INCREMENTAL IMPROVEMENT

I've always believed that growing a business was a process of incremental improvement—making the business a little bit better one day at a time. Unless there's some kind of outside influence that provides the opportunity to grow quickly, a business should grow and improve little by little. Improve the merchandise selection, improve the service, improve visual displays, and a thousand other things, and the business will grow and prosper.

But is incremental improvement enough to survive and thrive in a retail marketplace that's changing at breakneck speed, with new formats and new competitors cropping up every day? For the past several years we've been hearing the future belongs to those companies that move quickly. In my 35-plus years in the retail business, I've never seen so much change take place faster than it does now with eCommerce. The rules are being redefined so often that retailers have to rethink how they go about growing their businesses.

QUANTUM LEAPS!

Here's what I find most exciting about being in business today: It doesn't matter how big or small your company is or where you are located, as long as you bring something in the way of merchandise or a business concept to the marketplace that is unique and demonstrably superior. Then, there are lots of opportunities. Taking advantage of these opportunities means reevaluating how we think about our businesses.

STILL CRAZY AFTER ALL THESE YEARS

With respect to singer-songwriter Paul Simon, what I think retailing needs is a little more craziness, maybe a lot more. There are just too many boring stores, too much boring advertising, and too many retailers who are afraid to take chances and do what's being called "out-of-the-box" thinking.

I admit the phrase "out-of-the-box" is grossly overused, and there are too many experts running around telling everyone how they should embrace out-of-the-box thinking. I heard one famous so-called guru claim it was "the only way to transform your business into a truly customer-focused organization for the new millennium." This guy used every management-speak buzzword in the book while he proclaimed we should all get out of the box! But just saying you want to think out-of-the-box doesn't make it so. It requires some good, old craziness to foster innovation and creativity.

RADICAL THINKING

The concept of out-of-the-box thinking is sound, but I prefer to call it radical thinking. After all, some of the most innovative retail concepts came from truly radical thinkers. These radical thinkers may even have been called "crazy" somewhere along the line. I believe the marketplace is ready for some more radical thinking and some new radical kinds of retail stores and formats. Retailing needs some radical merchants such as Sol Price. When he created the first warehouse club, he defined a whole new industry segment.

We need more radical-thinking merchants like Jim McIngvale who turned the furniture business upside down in Houston because he thought there might be a better way. He wasn't afraid. He jumped in with both feet, worked his tail off, advertised like a wild man, and subscribed to the sound, business principles taught by Dr. W. Edwards Demming.

INNOVATION—ONE WAY TO BEAT THE BUSINESS CYCLE

It used to be a retailer could enjoy some success if the store was attractive and in a good location, merchandise selection was at least as good as that of the major competitors, service was at least as good, the store at least as convenient to shop, and the employees at least as attentive and helpful. To enjoy that same level of success in the marketplace of the future, "at least as" isn't enough. Stores and eCommerce sites that don't offer a unique and demonstrably superior shopping environment, merchandise selection, and compelling reasons for customers to shop there simply haven't got a chance.

The stock-market gyrations of late continue to shock the heart of the retail community and send a chill down the spines of many retailers. There is one thing every retailer knows with absolute certainty: The good times they have enjoyed through the late 1990s and early part of the 21st century will eventually lead to tougher periods as in the early 1990s. And one of the best ways I know to deal with and prepare for leaner times is to create an innovative environment. Foster an environment that encourages crazy ideas from crazy people who have an opportunity to voice ideas that don't mesh with the way everyone else is thinking. You've got to be different.

SOME CRAZY IDEAS!

- How would you like to have been in the room when someone at Sears brought up the idea of closing down their 100-year-old catalog operation? Crazy idea?

- How would you like to have been part of Jeff Bezos' brain trust when they decided to build a business called amazon.com selling books on the Internet? Crazy idea?

- How would you like to have been in the room when the two young men who conceived Teenage Mutant Ninja

Turtles tried to sell the concept to a New York advertising agency? Crazy idea?

• How would you like to have been in the dorm room when a couple of college students at Stanford dreamed up the idea for Yahoo? Crazy idea?

• How would you like to have been around when Kansas City developer J.C. Nichols conceived the first shopping center? Crazy idea?

• How would you like to have been around in 1939 when a Montgomery Ward copywriter developed Rudolph the Red-Nosed Reindeer for a promotion? Crazy idea?

• How would you like to have been the person who dreamed up QVC? Crazy idea?

Retailing needs more people with crazy ideas and the guts to do something about them.

NOW THAT YOU'VE READ MY THOUGHTS ON RETAIL SUCCESS, I CHALLENGE YOU TO ANSWER THESE FIVE QUESTIONS

1.
Do your stores, catalog, or Web site
define the category?

2.
Do you offer a unique and demonstrably
superior merchandise selection?

3.
Are you providing a shopping experience
that is so extraordinary as compared to the
competition that customers talk about
your store and tell their friends
how enjoyable it is to shop there?

4.
Are your employees more knowledgeable than
those in your competitors' stores?

5.
Are you considered the only ones
who do what you do?

INDEX

◆

ABOUT RETAIL MANAGEMENT CONSULTANTS

Retail Management Consultants, founded by George Whalin in 1987, provides services for retail organizations as well as consumer products manufacturers. With a focus on increasing sales and maximizing profits, services provided to retail organizations include:

- Strategic planning
- Operational evaluation
- Improving workforce performance through training and education
- The development of in-store merchandising programs
- Creation of business-building marketing programs

Services provided to consumer products manufacturers and wholesalers include:

- Customized sales and product training programs for retail salespeople
- Improvement of in-store positioning and merchandising of products

FOR MORE INFORMATION, CONTACT:

Retail Management Consultants

1635 S. Rancho Santa Fe Road, Suite 206
San Marcos, CA 92069
(800) 766-1908 or (760) 471-0207
Fax: (760) 471-0263

E-mail: info@whalinonretail.com
Web site: http://www.whalinonretail.com

GEORGE WHALIN'S SPEAKING SERVICES

George does keynotes and seminars for retailers, retail trade associations, consumer products manufacturers, and other related industry groups.

Up-to-date information on his topics can be found on his web site: www.whalinonretail.com.

George would love to hear your comments about *Retail Success!* His e-mail address is george@whalinonretail.com or call (800) 766-1908.

RETAIL SUCCESS!

Increase Sales, Maximize Profits, and Wow Your Customers in the Most Competitive Marketplace in History!

For additional copies of *Retail Success!*
visit our web site at www.whalinonretail.com
or call toll-free
(800) 766-1908

Quantity discounts are available.